Praise for Dave Barry Turns 50

"Riotous . . . [Barry] can find the humor in pretty much anything. And . . . he does not intend to go even slightly gently into that good night. . . . Barry's light-hearted, Everyman humor and what-me-worry grin have evoked comparisons with Mark Twain and Will Rogers, and earned him the Washington Post designation of America's Humorist."

—San Francisco Examiner

"Barry will prompt most baby boomers to laugh out loud. . . . His chapters on retirement planning and facing mortality are not only funny but right on. 'Right on'—you remember that phrase, don't you?"

—The Atlanta Journal-Constitution

"With age comes wisdom, among other ailments. [Barry's] no longer the happy-go-lucky, long-haired weirdo of his youth. Now the long hair sprouts from his ears. Getting older may be inevitable, but as Barry shows, there's no reason to take it with a straight face."

—BookPage

"It's the look back at TV commercials, politics, inventions, and attitudes that really makes those who have seen it all (much of 'it' through trifocals) chortle out loud. It's not unlike an archaeological dig through an attic, choking from laughter rather than dust, as familiar and forgotten memories are refreshed and taken for a satirical synaptic spin by a master humorist."

—Publishers Weekly

"Guess you'd better buy this book now while you can still read the print." —Library Journal

"A bushel of chuckles for readers." —Booklist

DAVE BARRY HITS BELOW THE BELTWAY

For Josh —
Happy Graduation!

Dave Bay

BALLANTINE BOOKS • NEW YORK

A Ballantine Book
Published by The Random House Ballantine Publishing Group
Copyright © 2001 by Dave Barry

www.ballantinebooks.com

ISBN 0-345-45919-9

This edition published by arrangement with Random House, Inc.

Manufactured in the United States of America

First Ballantine Books Trade Edition: November 2002
First Ballantine Books Mass Market Edition: May 2003

OPM 10 9 8 7 6 5 4 3 2 1

For Rob and Sophie,
mainly because I love them
more than I can say,
but also because someday
they will be paying for my Social Security

ACKNOWLEDGMENTS

FIRST AND FOREMOST, I thank the United States government for being the zany and wacky outfit that it is. I have long contended that, however many zillion dollars the federal government costs us, we get it all back and more in the form of quality entertainment.

I also thank my excellent Washington sources, especially Gene Weingarten, Tom Shroder, Joel Achenbach, Chuck Smith, and Russ Beland. What with one thing and another, I never got around to asking them for any actual information, but I know that, if I had, they would have tried to provide it. For that I am grateful.

I thank the many real journalists who do real stories about the federal government, thus providing me with fodder. I especially thank the journalists of *The Washington Post*, and my own paper, *The Miami Herald*, which, despite all the assaults by bean counters, still knows how to kick journalistic butt when it has to.

I thank my Research Department, Judi Smith, who fights an endless losing battle to make the things I write accurate, or at least less inaccurate. It is a tribute to her character that she has never, to my knowledge, turned to heroin.

Finally, I thank my editor, Sam Vaughan, and my agent, Al Hart, without whom I might have to get a real job.

CONTENTS

INTRODUCTION

To do even a halfway decent book on a subject as complex as the United States government, you have to spend a lot of time in Washington, D.C. So the first thing I decided, when I was getting ready to write this book, was that it would not be even halfway decent.

I decided this because I'm not comfortable in Washington. Don't get me wrong: Washington is a fine city, offering statues, buildings, and plenty of culture in the form of Thai restaurants. But when I'm in Washington, I always feel as though I'm the only person there who never ran for Student Council.

I started feeling this way back in 1967, when, as a college student, I got a job in Washington as a summer intern at *Congressional Quarterly*, a magazine that, as the name suggests, came out weekly.

I was totally unprepared for the Washington environment. I came from an all-male-college environment, where a person's standing in the community was judged on the basis of such factors as:

• Was he a good guy?
• Would he let you borrow his car?
• Would he still be your friend if your date threw up in his car?

But when I got to Washington I discovered that even among young people, being a good guy was not the key thing: The key thing was your position on the great Washington totem pole of status. Way up at the top of this pole is the president; way down at the bottom, below mildew, is the public. In between is an extremely complex hierarchy of government officials, journalists, lobbyists, lawyers, and other power players, holding thousands of minutely graduated status rankings differentiated by extremely subtle nuances that only Washingtonians are capable of grasping.

For example, Washingtonians know whether a person whose title is "Principal Assistant Deputy Undersecretary" is more or less important than a person whose title is "Associate Principal Deputy Assistant Secretary," or "Principal Deputy to Deputy Assistant Secretary," or "Deputy to the Deputy Secretary," or "Principal Assistant Deputy Undersecretary," or "Chief of Staff to the Assistant Assistant Secretary." (All of these are *real federal job titles*.)

Everybody in Washington always seems to know exactly how much status everybody else has. I don't know how they do it. Maybe they all get together in some secret location and sniff one another's rear ends. All I know is, back in my internship summer of 1967, when I went to Washington parties, they were nothing like parties I'd become used to in college. I was used to parties where it was not unusual to cap off the evening by drinking bourbon from a shoe, and not necessarily your *own* shoe. Whereas the Washington parties were *serious*. Everybody made an obvious effort to figure out where everybody else fit on the totem pole, and then spent the rest of the evening sucking up to whoever was higher up. I hated it. Of course, one reason for this was that nobody ever sucked up to me, since interns rank almost as low as members of the public.[1]

Today I have many good Washington friends, and I know that not everyone who lives there is a status-obsessed, butt-kissing toad. But there are still *way* too many people there who simply cannot get over how important they are. And do you want to know *why* they think they're important? Because they make policy! To the rest of America, making policy is a form of institutional masturbation; to Washingtonians, it is productive work. They *love* to make policy. They have policy out the wazoo. They can come up with a policy on *anything*, including the legal minimum size of the holes in Swiss cheese.[2]

---

[1] Insert your Monica Lewinsky suck-up joke here.

[2] In the final days of the administration of Bill "Legacy" Clinton, the U.S. Department of Agriculture issued a new standard under which the minimum size of the holes in Grade A Swiss was reduced to three eighths of an inch. Under the old standard, the holes had to be eleven sixteenths to thirteen sixteenths of an inch in diameter. I think we can all agree the world is now a better place.

A good depiction of the Washington worldview, I think, is the hit TV show *The West Wing*. Don't get me wrong: I think this show is well written, well acted, fast-paced, and entertaining. But Lordy, those characters are full of themselves, aren't they? They can't get *over* how important they are. They're so important that they can't even sit down. They're always striding briskly around the White House, striding striding striding, making policy with every step. We never see the bathrooms, but I suspect some of the characters stride while they pee.

Of course they rarely get a chance to go to the bathroom, because on *The West Wing*, they're always having a crisis. Like, in one episode I watched, the cast spent an hour hotly debating the question of whether the president should chide some environmental group for not condemning ecoterrorism. In other words, this issue was totally about words— whether the president should say harsh words to a group because that group had failed to say harsh words to another group. Nobody was talking about *doing* anything.

But to the characters on *The West Wing*, this was a very big, very dramatic deal. They were *anguishing* over it, while of course striding. Watching them, you cannot help but get caught up in the drama: Should the president chide? Or not chide? What would be the *repercussions* of the chiding? Should the president *stride* while chiding?

You forget that, outside of Washington, the vast majority of regular American taxpaying citizens truly do not care about things like this. The chiding issue is exactly the kind of hot-air, point-scoring, inside-politics nonevent that matters to Washington and four people at *The New York Times*, but that regular taxpaying Americans instinctively recognize as irrelevant to their lives. The reason you forget this is that regular taxpaying citizens are never depicted on shows like *The West Wing*. Presumably they're off doing some boring, nondramatic, non-policy-related thing, like working.

Anyway, my point is that, even though this book is largely about the federal government, I spent very little time doing research in Washington, or for that matter anywhere else. I mainly sat around and made stuff up. So if you were concerned about encountering a lot of actual information in this book, relax! There's almost none. To compensate for the lack of facts, I have included a great many snide remarks.[3]

That is not to say that this book is useless. On the contrary, I believe you will find that, of all the books ever written about the United States government and political system, this book contains, by far, the largest number of illustrations involving zucchini. And maybe—just maybe—somewhere in this book you'll find some tidbit that will actually inform you, and help you to be a better citizen!

If you do, please let me know, so I can eliminate that tidbit from the next edition.

---

[3]If you want a book about government that is both factual and snide, I strongly recommend P. J. O'Rourke's excellent *Parliament of Whores*.

CHAPTER ONE

The Origins of Government (or)

Defending Humanity from Giant Carnivorous Vegetables

WHY DO WE HAVE GOVERNMENT?

This is a hard question, and, like so many hard questions, the best way to answer it is to consider ants. When you see an ant on your kitchen floor, it appears to be an insignificant insect scurrying around randomly, so you stomp it into a little smear without a second thought.

But if, instead of stomping on the ant, you were to get down on your hands and knees and *follow* it, something fascinating would happen: Your head would bonk into the wall, because the ant has scurried into a hole. So I'll just tell you where the ant goes: It goes to a nest containing an ant colony that is every bit as complex and organized as human society. In fact, it is *more* organized, because there are no teenagers.

Yes, even ants—tiny creatures with a primitive

brain no larger than that of a psychic-hotline caller—have a government. The ant government operates on what political scientists call the "Smell System," whereby your role in society is based on what chemicals you secrete. At the top of the hierarchy is the queen, who is elected unanimously by the other ants after a very brief political campaign that consists of hatching.

"Hey!" the other ants say. "This smells like the queen!"

Most of the other ants smell like workers, so they spend their lives scurrying around looking for food and exchanging important chemical information with the other ants they bump into ("I'm an ant!" "Hey! Me too!"). Also, there are a few winged ants, whose job is to scare you by flying around your house pretending to be termites. (This is the only form of entertainment that ants have.)

Ants are not the only animals that have government. Similar organizational structures can be found throughout nature: Monkeys form troops, birds form flocks, fish form schools, worms form bunches of worms, intestinal parasites form law firms, etc. In other words: *Governments are natural.* All animals form them, including humans. In a way, we are like the ants scurrying across our kitchen floor: We give our Cheez-It fragments (tax money) to the colony (government), and in return we enjoy the many benefits provided by the colony (the Federal Avocado Safety Administration).

Of course human beings are far more advanced than animals; we do not elect the president of the United States based on how he smells. As cerebral beings, we are much more interested in other qualities in our president, such as height. As a result, we here in the United States have developed a sophisticated, highly complex government structure involving three major branches.[1] (Among other animal species, only woodpeckers have more.)

In this book, we will be taking a detailed look at the modern United States government—where it came from, what it does, who works for it, what planet they originated on, etc. But to truly understand how our government works in twenty-first-century America, we must travel millions of years back in time and examine:

Early Human Governments

The first humans were short, hairy, tree-dwelling creatures that strongly resembled Danny DeVito. Like their close genetic cousins, the apes, the humans lived in trees and had developed opposable thumbs. What distinguished the humans was that after sitting around in their trees for a couple million years with pretty much nothing to do except scratch themselves, they had made the most important discovery in the history of the world, the discovery that would vault them past all other animals: how to make the sign as we see in Exhibit A:

Exhibit A

[1] The Executive, the Legislative, and the Deceased.

This discovery of the "OK" sign gave the humans a huge strategic advantage over the apes, who could only make a noncommittal shrugging gesture, as shown in Exhibit B:

This meant that if a smart ape thought up a good idea, such as the wheel, the other apes—even if they were really impressed—could only shrug, and the smart ape would think, "Ah, the hell with it."

Exhibit B

The primitive humans, on the other hand, used their new OK! sign to respond to pretty much anything anybody did. This encouraged progress. And so on the historic day when one of the humans was considering the idea of leaving his tree and roaming around on the ground, the other humans went: OK!

Thus emboldened, the courageous explorer stepped down onto the ground. It was a momentous moment in human history, comparable to when astronaut Neil Armstrong first set foot on the moon, except that instead of saying, "That's one small step for man, one giant leap for mankind," the courageous early explorer said "Urk," because a passing mastodon had stomped him into a smear. The other humans, seeing this, made the OK! sign to one another and remained in the trees, where they decided that, to protect themselves, they had better form a government.

The system they came up with—humanity's first

form of government—was the Tribal System. The leader was chosen via the following process:

1. The tribe would hold a council, called the Sacred Council, wherein all the adult males would sit in a circle, called the Circle of Deciding, and decide, by consensus, which one of them was the most wise, trustworthy, and brave. This member would be designated as the Chosen One.
2. The Chosen One would pick up a stout stick, called the Staff of Authority, and hold it aloft, asking the gods for guidance.
3. While the Chosen One was doing this, he would get his head bashed in by the Great Big Rock of Heaviness, which was wielded by the male with the biggest muscles, who would then be unanimously elected leader.

These early humans needed a strong government leader, because their lives were harsh. They were hunter-gatherers, which meant that the men would go out and hunt wild game, after which the women would gather up the men's remaining body parts, because the game back then was *really* wild.

Even when the humans did manage to kill an animal, they had to eat it raw. This situation continued for several eons, until one lucky day when a primitive human—we'll call him Oog[2]—happened to be standing outside during a thunderstorm, holding a piece of mammoth meat, and was struck by light-

[2]Name changed for legal reasons.

ning. When the smoke cleared, the other humans tasted the now-cooked mammoth meat, and they discovered that it tasted much better. They also discovered that Oog was delicious.

This discovery ushered in what archaeologists call the Age of Barbecue. When the tribe killed an animal, the tribal leader would designate one unfortunate person as the Meat Holder. This person had to stand outside during thunderstorms, holding the meat in the air on a stick (*see drawing*) while the other tribe members waited safely inside a cave until they heard lightning strike, indicating that their food was done.

Ancient Cave Drawing Depicting Cooking During the Age of Barbecue
(Source: A Cave)

This brutal system finally came to an end when the humans discovered that they could create their own fire whenever they wanted by simply rubbing sticks together. This enabled them to have light and heat inside the cave while they waited for lightning to strike the Meat Holder.

The Age of Barbecue lasted for 1.2 million years, during which the human race gradually developed a powerful hankering for side dishes. This in turn led to the invention of agriculture.

Early agriculture was very labor-intensive: Workers toiled endlessly at the backbreaking labor of clearing and tilling[3] the fields by hand. Then they'd spend anxious months praying for rain, chasing off pests, staring at the field, and hoping that their crops would grow—only to be bitterly disappointed time and again. This went on for 285,000 years, at which point somebody came up with the idea of planting seeds in the field.

This breakthrough brought both good news and bad news:

- The good news was, the seeds worked.
- The bad news was, these particular seeds were for zucchini.

Primitive Human Flees Herd of Giant Prehistoric Zucchini
(Artist's Conception)

[3]Whatever the hell "tilling" is.

Within a matter of hours, huge, violent prehistoric zucchini weighing up to nine hundred pounds per unit were erupting from the ground, forcing the primitive humans to flee to other continents, thus spreading the human race around the world.

Eventually, humans learned to grow less hostile crops, such as corn, maize,[4] and alfalfa.[5] They also learned to make simple tools, such as the plow, the adze,[6] and the level.[7] A few tribes had begun to try to domesticate animals, although the results were sometimes less than beneficial, as evidenced by the badly gnawed skeletal remains of one tribe that apparently attempted to attach its plows to teams of squirrels. The first animals to be successfully domesticated were dogs, which were a big help because they would bark all night and fetch thrown sticks,[8] thereby freeing humans from having to perform these tedious yet vital tasks.

The next important technological development was the discovery of iron, which resulted in the Iron Age, followed about six months later by the Rust Age. This new metal technology led to the Era of a Lot of Fighting, as the tribes with arrows and spears made of solid metal found that they could easily defeat those tribesmen using cardboard with aluminum foil wrapped around it.

As the more powerful tribes began to conquer

[4]Corn.

[5]We still grow this, but nobody remembers why.

[6]An ax-like instrument used as an answer in crossword puzzles.

[7]This was basically just a stone that was used to whack things or people until they were level.

[8]But not give them back.

other tribes and control larger areas of land, civilizations formed. The first big one was in Egypt, which grew into a large nation and then declined, as shown in the historical map sequence below.

The Egyptian form of government was headed by the pharaohs,[9] who were worshiped as gods; they had absolute power and could do whatever they wanted. As you would imagine, they had an extensive intern program.

When the pharaohs died, they turned into mummies, a constant threat because they'd creep around

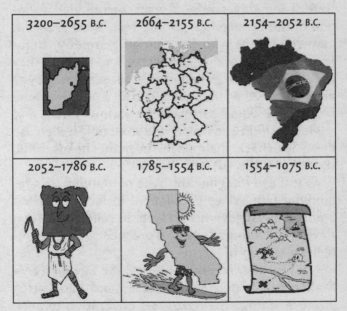

Growth and Decline of Ancient Egypt
(Source: The American Dental Association)

[9]This word never looks like it's spelled right.

at night and scare the bejabbers[10] out of people. To prevent this from happening, the Egyptians buried the mummies deep inside pyramids, which were history's first public works projects.

Today, when we look at these massive structures, we ask ourselves in wonderment: How the heck did the Egyptians *do* this? How could an ancient civilization—one that did not possess even rudimentary bulldozers—manage to pile these massive blocks of stone on top of one another?

The answer is: mathematics. The Egyptians, despite living thousands of years before the invention of the Scholastic Aptitude Test, were excellent mathematicians who understood geometry, trigonometry, long division, the cosine, and tipping. They used this knowledge to harness the awesome power of leverage. When they needed to lift a massive stone block, they would calculate the various forces and angles, fashion tree trunks into stout poles, then use these to whack their slaves over the heads while shouting: "PICK UP THIS BLOCK!"

As you can imagine, this type of mathematics required a large slave population. In fact, from that point on, most government systems relied heavily on slaves to get things done; this practice continued until the discovery of taxpayers.

Anyway, after several centuries, the Egyptian civilization finally declined because sand had gotten into everything. The next great civilization to arise was Ancient Greece, which came up with an exciting

[10]The Egyptians invented the bejabber, which was the forerunner to the modern bejeeper.

new governing concept called "democracy," from the Greek words *dem*, meaning "everybody gets to vote," and *ocracy*, meaning "except of course women, slaves, and poor people."

The Ancient Greeks produced some great thinkers, including Socrates, Jimmy the Ancient Greek, and Plato, the brilliant teacher who founded the most influential school of the ancient world.[11] Plato's top student was Aristotle, who invented logic, which meant that for the first time, it was possible to prove things by means of a device called a "syllogism," whereby you would make two statements and then draw a conclusion, as in this example:

1. Some toads are poisonous.
2. Marlon Brando looks increasingly like a toad.
3. Therefore, you probably should not eat Marlon Brando.

With this powerful new tool, the Greeks, led by their legendary military genius Alexander "the Great" Onassis, became a world power. They'd march into a foreign country and start arguments with the foreigners, who did not have the syllogism and thus were easily defeated. But fate turned against the Greeks in 432 B.C., when their rivals, the Spartans, invented sarcasm. This was a formidable counterweapon. The Greeks would make their statements and give their conclusion, and the Spartans would just go, "Yeah, right." Within hours the Greek

[11]Harvard.

empire collapsed, creating a void that was soon filled by what would ultimately become the greatest, most powerful, most feared, and most influential empire that the world had ever seen: the New York Yankees.

No, sorry, we're getting ahead of ourselves. The next major empire was of course the Romans, who were headquartered in Rome, Italy. The Romans were an amazing people who had somehow learned how to speak Latin and invented many important abbreviations—including "etc.," "ibid.," "OK," and "R.S.V.P."—that are still in use today. They also had a large, powerful, highly disciplined army that wore coordinated outfits consisting of sandals, skirts, and helmets with brushes on them. The Roman soldiers would march into a foreign territory, and while the foreigners were rolling around on the ground, laughing and shouting sarcastic remarks such as "Oh *please* don't hurt me, Mister Brush-Helmet Man!" the Romans would stab them with spears. By

Roman Soldiers Driving Giant Prehistoric Zucchini Out of Europe

this process they were able to conquer most of Europe and drive out the last remaining herds of giant marauding prehistoric zucchini.

This created a *pax romana*[12] that lasted for several hundred years, during which the Romans, utilizing the innovative engineering technique of poking spears into slaves, built roads, aqueducts, shopping malls, etc. By this point they were operating under a system of government known technically as the "Fat Guys Wearing Bedsheets System." This was a *quid pro quo*[13] type of arrangement, under which the residents of the empire sent the vast majority of their wealth to Rome, where it was consumed by fat guys wearing bedsheets.

In exchange, the residents of the empire got: more fat guys wearing bedsheets.

Ultimately, the Roman empire was doomed to fall, because for some insane reason it used Roman numerals, and nobody could remember what "L" stood for.[14] As a result the Romans wasted many hours standing around arguing about how much everything cost. While they were thus preoccupied, barbarian tribes including the Huns, the Goths, the Visigoths, the Ostrogoths, and the Goth Darnits swept down from the north in horde formation and, despite the brave defensive efforts of the Roman soldiers, caused the Roman empire to collapse.

With civilization destroyed, humanity sank into the Dark Ages. This was a bad time, lasting about

[12]Literally, "period that lasts for several hundred years."
[13]This doesn't mean anything.
[14]They were not so sure about "C" either.

Barbarian Hordes Take Over Roman Empire

one thousand years, during which hardly anybody read books and there was widespread ignorance. It was a lot like now, only without TV.

The system of government used during the Dark Ages was "feudalism," because it was based on feuding. The main feud was between the Christians and the Muslims over the Holy Land. From time to time a group of Christians would organize a Crusade and march all the way to the Middle East to reclaim the Holy Land, and they'd be gone for maybe five years, and then finally they'd come straggling back shouting, "We got it! We got the Holy Land!" And all the other Christians would gather around, and the Crusaders would display: a box of dirt. And the other Christians would say, "That's it?" And the Crusaders would get all defensive and reply, "Hey, *you* see how much Holy Land you can carry across a whole darned continent!"

So they'd put the Holy Land on display, and in a couple of months, what with normal spillage and people taking souvenirs, it would be pretty much gone, and somebody would have to organize *another* Crusade. As you can imagine, this required money, which was provided by a revenue-garnering system based on serfs, who tilled[15] the soil in exchange for not getting their limbs lopped off with swords. Administering this system was a hierarchy of officials headed by the king, as shown in the chart below.

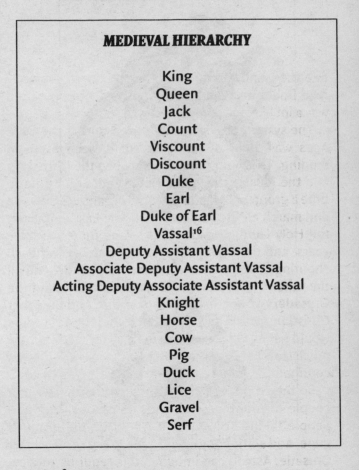

MEDIEVAL HIERARCHY

King
Queen
Jack
Count
Viscount
Discount
Duke
Earl
Duke of Earl
Vassal[16]
Deputy Assistant Vassal
Associate Deputy Assistant Vassal
Acting Deputy Associate Assistant Vassal
Knight
Horse
Cow
Pig
Duck
Lice
Gravel
Serf

[15]See footnote 3.
[16]These people were not popular; hence the term "What a vassal!"

The society was organized around units of land called fiefdoms, with each fiefdom measuring a certain number[17] of hectares per rood of cubit. At the center of each fiefdom was a castle, which had a

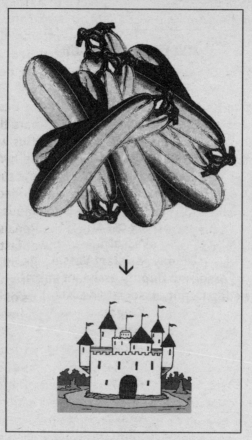

Catapult Zucchini Attack on Castle
(Source: Soldier of Fortune)

[17]Usually 614.

moat around it and a drawbridge that would be raised whenever a boat had to go through.

Sometimes two fiefdoms would get into a feud, and soldiers from one of them would march over to the other one's castle and lay siege to it. They would use various techniques to try to make the castle occupants surrender, including shooting flaming arrows, singing "A Hundred Bottles of Beer on the Wall"[18] all the way through, or knocking on the castle door and pretending to be delivering pizza.

If these techniques didn't work, the besiegers would sometimes use catapults to bombard the castle with boulders, diseased cattle, or—this weapon is often referred to by historians as "the hydrogen bomb of the Dark Ages"—giant prehistoric zucchini.

So the Dark Ages were a brutal time indeed, but they finally ended in 1483, when the famous Italian person Leonardo da Vinci invented the Renaissance. This ushered in an era when humanity at last awakened from the long restless sleep of unenlightenment, brushed the slimy bad-tasting film of ignorance from its teeth, excreted the waste products of intolerance from its bladder, and wiped the eye boogers of anti-intellectualism from its eyes.

Within hours, nation-states began to form, the main ones being England, France, Holland, Britain, Spain, the Dutch, Portugal, the Netherlands, the Ottoman Empire, and maize. All of these nation-states wanted to engage in trade so they could get spices, which were a very hot commodity back then and are often referred to by historians as "the Internet stocks

---

[18]This song is the earliest known example of disco.

of the fifteenth century." This resulted in an Age of Exploration, in which hardy mariners set out on tiny ships to discover the rest of the world. This took tremendous courage, because when we say "tiny ships," we are not exaggerating, as shown in this illustration:

Early Sailing Ship
(Shown Actual Size)

The hardy mariners would step onto these ships and instantly sink like hardy stones into the sea, where they would fall prey to sharks or giant sea-going zucchini.[19]

Eventually the mariners figured out that they should make the ships bigger. They were then able to reach the Orient, where they would pick up a load of spices, then begin the arduous return journey. These perilous voyages sometimes took years, at the end of which the mariners would return triumphantly to their home port, to be greeted at the dock by excited throngs of their countrymen shouting, "You got *nut-meg*? The recipe says *oregano*, you morons!"

Nevertheless, the trading nations grew in wealth. Your typical nation in those days had a monarchy system of government, under which all the wealth, after expenses, was divided up equally, and then turned over to the king. The king would use the

[19]If you think we're getting tired of the zucchini joke, you had best think again.

wealth to provide his nation with the fundamental elements of government: a palace, a summer palace, a winter palace, a guest palace, a hunting palace, a lot of palace furniture, many paintings of the king, and some mechanism for chopping off people's heads.

Also of course each nation would have a big army, because in those days kings were always getting into huge complicated grudge-based wars with one another. A good example was the Hundred Years' War, in which England and France fought for over a century over the commercial rights to Flanders, only to discover after most of their soldiers were dead that neither side had a clue where (or what) "Flanders" was (or were).[20] You can imagine the hearty royal laugh they had over that "boo-boo"!

As the trading nations of Western Europe gained in power, it began to occur to them that, instead of trading with other continents, there would be real financial advantages involved in actually *owning* them, so they took possession of Africa, North America, and South America. It turned out that there were people already living on these continents, but they were primitive people who could not even speak English. They were happy to give up their land, natural resources, and freedom in exchange for the benefits of civilization, such as not getting shot.

At first the Europeans were mainly interested in removing all the valuables from their new colonies, particularly gold and silver, which were highly prized in those days and are often referred to by historians

[20]It turns out that there is no such thing.

as "the Pokémon cards of the fifteenth and sixteenth centuries." But eventually Europeans began to create permanent settlements in the colonies. One such group was the Pilgrims, who were unpopular in England because of their belief in a stern, unbending God who wanted them to wear hats shaped like traffic cones. In 1620, the Pilgrims sailed from England to Massachusetts, and during that long, difficult, storm-tossed crossing, they wrote and signed the historic Mayflower Compact,[21] which states: "Boy, are *we* nauseous."

The Mayflower Compact also set forth a new concept of government, under which the colonists— instead of ceding authority to some faraway king— would make their own decisions for themselves, as free men, able to control their own destinies. Most of them were dead by spring. But the ones who survived were able, with the help of a friendly Native American named Squanto,[22] to grow enough food to survive the next winter, and that fall they held the first Thanksgiving to watch football and celebrate the bountiful harvest.

Yes, life was looking good for the Pilgrims. But big changes were looming on the horizon. Because these colonists had dared to squeeze the tube of independence, thus releasing the toothpaste of self-rule, and there was to be no putting it back. The stage was being set, in this new world, for a new kind of government—a courageous and noble experiment in human coexistence that would lead to the

[21]Named for their ship, the *Compact*.
[22]Literally, "He Who Squants."

The First Thanksgiving
(Source: Annie Leibovitz)

creation of the greatest power that the world has ever known: Microsoft. In the next chapter, we'll examine the origins of this great corporation as well as its host nation, the United States. It is a fascinating saga, and one that we hope to God is zucchini-free.[23]

[23]But we would not bet on it.

CHAPTER TWO

The United States Is Born (or)

The Spirit of Freedom Wakes Up and Smells the Heifers

AFTER THE PILGRIMS reached the New World in the previous chapter, a number of very significant historical events occurred, and before you knew it the year was 1765. At this point, the area that was to become the United States consisted of thirteen colonies—or, as they proudly referred to themselves in promotional brochures, "The Thirteen *Original* Colonies."[1]

What was life like in the colonies? Probably the best word to describe it would be "colonial." An estimated 83 percent of the population lived on farms,[2] which meant that for a typical family of four, the day

---

[1]Massachusetts, Pennsylvania, Virginia, West Virginia, Maryland, the Colony Next to Maryland, New York, Upstate New York, Brooklyn, Queens, Alaska, Hawaii, and the Netherlands.

[2]Source: an unusually vivid dream.

began at 4:30 A.M. with the crowing of the rooster. Brushing the sleep from his eyes, Pa would climb out of bed, walk wearily to the doorway, and—as generations of farmers had done before him—fire a shot at the rooster. Unfortunately, most firearms in those days were highly inaccurate, so more often than not Pa would hit the cow. The resulting high-pitched moo of chagrin would rouse the rest of the family. The farm day had begun!

As Pa headed outside with his pitchfork to hunt for the rooster, Ma would rouse the kids, Johnny and Sarah Jane, and they would begin daily chores, while Ma, knowing that the entire household depended on her skill and diligence, sneaked back to bed, which is where she kept her fermented dandelion juice. Johnny would go out to milk the cow, which was not easy if the cow was dead, which on many mornings it was. Meanwhile Sarah Jane would light the stove and cook up a hearty farm breakfast of eggs, bacon, sausage, grits, biscuits, giblets,[3] hotcakes, oatmeal, corn bread, pork chops, roast filet of squirrel, and reduced-fat ham hocks, all of which she would eat herself. (Sarah Jane weighed 375 pounds.)

By now the sun had risen and the serious work of farming had begun. Pa would put the harness on Old Dobbin,[4] head out to the back forty, and resume the seemingly endless task of pulling out rocks and tree stumps. It was brutally hard work, but Pa kept going day after day in the grueling sun, because he had a dream—a dream that some day, that rocky, stump-

[3]These are small gibs.
[4]Their slave.

strewn piece of ground would be transformed into a lush and fertile field, where he would grow corn and wheat and garnish-grade parsley, which he would be able to sell for cash money, which he would use to buy a better rifle or maybe even a cannon so he could kill *the damned rooster*. Pa's dream was shared by many colonial farmers, including Pa's neighbor, who, unbeknownst to Pa, was the legal owner of the back forty. Pa actually owned the *front* forty, but he had read his deed incorrectly, although the neighbor did not plan to point this out until Pa finished removing all the rocks and stumps.

While Pa cleared the field, Johnny would head out to the pasture and round up the heifers. Then he'd stand there the rest of the day, shifting nervously from foot to foot, because Pa had never told him what he was supposed to *do* with the heifers, and Johnny was afraid to ask. Meanwhile Sarah Jane would sit at the spinning wheel, thereby causing the stool to collapse like a Dixie cup under a Chevrolet Suburban, leaving Sarah Jane with no choice but to waddle back over to the stove and prepare herself a hearty traditional farm lunch.

Come nightfall, the entire family would gather in the kitchen for an evening of togetherness, except for Ma, who was in bed with a headache; and Johnny, still cowering in the pasture, surrounded by heifers; and Pa, who was crouching outside in the bushes, holding an ax and making what he believed to be the sounds of a chicken in heat. This meant the job of polishing off the traditional hearty farm supper fell entirely to Sarah Jane, who many a night fell asleep, exhausted, with her head still inside the butter churn.

Yes, the colonial lifestyle was harsh and unforgiving, and far too often it was cut short by accidents or heifer-transmitted diseases. But it was a lifestyle that had produced a population of hardy, independent, self-reliant people who did not cotton to highfalutin ways.

And that meant that there was trouble brewing on the horizon, because the Thirteen Original Colonies legally belonged to Britain, which at that time was a hotbed of falutin. It was ruled by a king who went by the moniker of King George III. He thought he was better than everybody else and made no bones about it.5

King George III
(Source: The British Museum)

But the real power in Britain was in the hands of Parliament, which was divided into two houses, the House of Lords and the House of Lords Phase II. Both houses were made up of wealthy degenerates who wore tights and inherited their money and would not have recognized a heifer if they woke up in bed with one, which they often did.

In 1765, Parliament passed the Stamp Act, which, as any American high school student can tell you, was an act that apparently had something to do with stamps. As you can imagine, the colonists did

5Does anybody have *any* idea what this expression means?

not cotton[6] to this one little bit. They were darned if they were going to be told what to do with their stamps by a bunch of tights-wearing heifer-lovers all the way over in England. So a group of them formed a secret organization called the Sons of Liberty and began holding clandestine meetings to protest the Stamp Act. After several months it began to dawn on them that, since they were meeting in secret, nobody had any idea that they were protesting.

So they started meeting in public, and the Stamp Act was finally repealed, only to be replaced by the Townshend Acts, which were not only harder to spell, but also included a tax on tea. This *really* got the colonists' dander up. Today it is hard for us to imagine Americans feeling so strongly about tea, but we must understand that back in those simpler times—when there were no soft drinks, bottled water, or other prepackaged beverages—"tea" was slang for marijuana.

And so it was that on the night of December 16, 1773, a band[7] of brave men dressed themselves as Native Americans, went down to Boston Harbor, where three tea-laden British ships were anchored, and—striking a bold blow for liberty—dropped giant prehistoric zucchini on them.

This made Parliament so mad it could spit. In retaliation, it passed a set of hugely unpopular acts that became known as the Hugely Unpopular Acts—

---

[6]When you get down to brass tacks, the colonists did not do much cottoning.

[7]The Standells.

The Boston Tea Party
(Source: Department of Defense)

brutally punitive measures that threatened the colonists with imprisonment if they removed their mattress tags, and forced them to change the time on all their clocks twice a year for no coherent reason.

This was, to quote from the work of the great writer and philosopher Thomas Paine, "bad." On March 19, 1775, with tension mounting to the boiling point, British troops marched from Boston to the rural towns of Lexington and Concord, where, in a military drama that will reverberate forever on the big gong of history, they realized that the battles of Lexington and Concord were not scheduled to take place until

April 19, 1775. So they marched back to Boston, and a month later the Revolutionary War began.

From that point various things continued to happen until July 4, 1776, when the Founding Fathers celebrated the Fourth of July by signing the Declaration of Independence, a sacred document that is kept in a secure, climate-controlled vault in the National Archives at all times except for a couple of instances when the Clinton administration let campaign donors wear it to parties as a hat. We cherish the Declaration because it expresses, in the timeless prose of its author, Francis "Scott" Key, the ideals upon which this great nation was founded:

> Whereas in the course of human events it behooves us, the people, not to ask, What can our country do for us, anyway? but rather, whether we have anything to fear except fear itself, so that a government of the people, by the people, and for the people, may be one nation, under God, who art in heaven, as we forgive those who trespass against us and solemnly swear to tell the truth, the whole truth, and nothing but the truth until death do us part as long as we both shall live or 75,000 miles, whichever comes first, amen.

Even today, when we read these words, we are struck physically in the head by how meaningful they are. What the Founding Fathers were saying, basically, was: "Why should we let people over in England saddle us with an unresponsive government and stupid laws? We can create our own!"

But first they had to finish fighting the Revolutionary War, a long, bitter, and complex struggle that we will not discuss in detail here because that would require research. The important thing is that when the British finally surrendered in 1781 following the Battle of Gettysburg, the colonists were at last free to form a new nation, which they decided to name "The United States of America," in recognition of the fact that "Luxembourg" was taken.

The next order of business was to come up with a system of government. The first one they tried, from 1781 through 1787, was called the "Articles of Confederation,"[8] and it basically, to quote the always wise and pithy Benjamin Franklin, "sucked." The problem was that the federal government was very weak; for example, the entire U.S. armed forces consisted of a dog named Jasper. Foreign powers soon realized that they could defeat the United States via the military tactic of shouting "DOWN, boy!"

So the Founding Fathers decided that they had to come up with something better, and in 1787 they met in Philadelphia and, after much debate, created the document that would become the blueprint for our nation: *Moby-Dick*.

No, seriously, they created the United States Constitution. This incredible document is the basis for

[8]Author: Strom Thurmond.

all of the fundamental rights that we enjoy as Americans, such as the right to throw away our third-class mail without opening it. And yet, incredible as it may seem, most Americans have *never read the Constitution*. Many Americans don't even know what the Constitution is, as was shown in a recent Gallup poll in which 54 percent of the respondents identified it as "maybe a hockey team."

How can this be? How can Americans know so little about what is undoubtedly the most significant political document ever created? One reason, of course, is that a great many Americans are stupid. There is no other explanation for the wildly enthusiastic reception that this nation gave to the Taco Bell chihuahua.

But another reason why many Americans have never read the Constitution is that it has never been presented to them in a clear, readable format. So here it is, your Constitution, the entire document, including the rarely seen footnotes.

The Constitution of the
United States of America

Preamble

WE THE PEOPLE OF THE UNITED STATES, in order to form a more perfect union, establish justice, insure domestic tranquillity, use the word "emoluments," etc., do hereby and forthwith set forth the document hereinafter referred to as the Constitution of the United States of America.

Article I

Section 1

The Legislative Branch shall consist of a Congress consisting of a Senate and a House of Representatives, which shall cancel each other out.

Section 2

The House of Representatives shall be composed of people who own at least two dark suits and have not been indicted recently. They shall be elected every two years following a campaign lasting two years, and they shall continue being elected forever as long as they can continue to provide their districts with massive unnecessary highway projects paid for by taxpayers from other districts.

Section 3

The Senate shall be composed of people who wish to be President and have developed a Vision for America in the form of at least three media consultants.

Section 4

If anything ever happens, anywhere in the world, every member of both Houses of Congress shall issue a press release about it within two working minutes. Then there shall be hearings.

Section 5

A bill shall become a law when both houses of Congress have added massive unnecessary highway projects to it, and it has been signed by the President in an elaborate White House ceremony wherein all parties involved claim full credit for every positive thing that has ever happened to the human race, including the discovery of fire.

Section 6

Congress shall also create a Tax Code weighing more than the combined poundage of the largest member of the House and the largest member of the Senate, plus a standard musk ox.

Section 7

If Congress finds out that any normal citizen can actually understand any sentence of the Tax Code, then that sentence shall immediately be returned to the Joint Committee on Emoluments for further wordification.

Section 8

Section 8 has been intentionally left blank.

Section 9

If any member of Congress is caught stealing or committing murder or passing out naked next to a stripper in the Capitol Rotunda, then that member shall accuse the opposing political party of "partisanship."

Section 10

Congress shall have the power to punish piracy on the high seas.

Section 11

Piracy on the low seas is OK.

Article II

Section 1

There shall be an executive branch consisting of the President of the United States, who shall be a tallish man; and the First Lady of the United States, who shall be a woman who is married to the President and has a sincere concern for children and plenty of hairspray.

There shall also be a Vice President, but the Constitution frankly does not know why.

The President shall be elected every four years according to the following procedure:

(a) In the dead of winter, all interested candidates and their entourages, as well as members of the national press corps on expense accounts, shall go to Iowa and New Hampshire, unless somebody discovers two states that are even more wretched places to spend the dead of winter.

(b) The candidates shall go around shaking hands with the residents of these states while voicing passionate concern for their local problems, their children, their schools, their pigs, etc. The candidates shall keep this up until they have shaken every resident's hand at least twice and secretly wish that giant volcanoes would erupt in Des Moines and Manchester and bury both states under fifty feet of hot lava.

(c) During this period, nobody in the entire rest of the United States, other than Washington, D.C., and its immediate environs, shall give a rat's ass.

(d) When the citizens of Iowa and New Hampshire are suffering widespread Repetitive Stress Syndrome from shaking hands with candidates pretending to care about them, primary elections or caucuses[9] shall be held. The instant that the votes are counted, the candidates, entourages, and press corps members shall vacate these two states faster than Senator Ted Kennedy vacates a submerged Oldsmobile.

(e) At this point each major party shall have at least one Front-runner who is obviously going to win, and one Surprise Challenger who is obviously not going to win, but who shall get a huge amount of attention from the press corps because without some kind of contest there would be no good reason for the press corps to be traipsing around the nation on expense accounts. The Candidates and the Surprise Challengers shall spend the next several months conducting primary campaigns in which they shall:

---

[9]We have no idea what "caucusing" is, and we wrote the Constitution.

1. Heatedly denounce special interests, and

2. Raise millions of dollars from special interests.

(ƒ) In the armpit of summer, when the sun is causing urban fire hydrants to melt, each major party shall hold a convention in a big-city convention center surrounded by heavy police security and random loony protesters fighting for causes such as voting rights for mollusks. At this convention—which shall feature speeches by every living human who has ever served in the rank of lieutenant governor or above, and which shall garner lower TV ratings than an infomercial for a do-it-yourself circumcision device[10]—the delegates shall nominate the Front-runner, who shall then be warmly endorsed by the Surprise Challenger, despite the fact that he has spent the past six months loudly declaring to the world that the Front-runner makes Hitler look like Captain Kangaroo.

(g) There shall then be a fall election campaign in which each candidate shall:

1. Call on his opponent to "avoid sleazy personal attacks" and "talk about the issues," and

2. Run commercials implying that his opponent is a bribe-taking criminal sex pervert who favors the shooting of Social Security recipients for sport.

(h) At around the time of the World Series, a few members of the actual voting public will start to figure out that something is going on involving

[10]The Ronco Whack-o-Matic.

politics. "Hey," they shall ask one another, "are we having an election or something?"

(i) On the first Tuesday of November, those voters who have not been rendered physically ill by the campaign shall go to the polls and elect the candidate who is, in their opinion, taller.

(j) All World Series games shall be held in the daytime. It says so right here in the Constitution, and anybody who violates this law should be executed without trial.

(k) Also, notice there is nothing in here about any so-called Electoral College.

Section 2

The President shall be Commander in Chief of the Armed Forces and shall give a snappy military salute to the guard when getting into or out of his helicopter. If the President is unfamiliar with saluting because his total military experience consists of having once owned a G.I. Joe action figure, he shall practice in front of a mirror.

Section 3

The President shall never go anywhere, including the Dairy Queen, without a motorcade the length of Chile.

Section 4

If any football, baseball, or basketball team wins a national championship, the President shall invite the team members to the White House for some manly handshaking.

Section 5

Every six months, the President shall get delegates from Israel and one of Israel's neighboring nations to meet in some unknown dirtball little burg in Maryland or West Virginia that has no decent restaurants, and he shall make them stay there until they sign a Historic Peace Accord, which shall have the life span of a duck in a trash compactor.

Section 6

In the event of a massive natural disaster such as a drought or flood, the President shall put on a polo shirt and get into a helicopter and fly over the devastated area and frown down on it with concern, after which he shall hug some victims and declare that, sure enough, a disaster has occurred. It would be pretty funny if, just once, the President said, "Hey, that didn't look so bad!" But the President shall never do this.

Section 7

The President shall have interns, in case he needs a pizza or whatever.

Article III

Section 1

The highest court in the land shall be the Supreme Court, which shall consist of nine justices who exhibit at least some sign of life, such as twitching when jabbed with a hatpin.

Section 2

From time to time the Supreme Court shall take a stab at resolving the abortion question, but forget about it.

Section 3

Members of the Supreme Court shall be butt-naked under their robes.

Article IV

Section 1

There shall be a bunch of States.

Section 2

Each State shall be governed by a Governor who would like to be President and a State Legislature consisting of individuals considered too marginal even to be members of Congress.

Section 3

Each State shall have an Official State Motto, Song, Tree, Flower, Bird, Mineral, Vegetable, Reptile, Soil, Parasite, Barbecue Recipe, and Tourism Promotion Slogan, such as "Arkansas: Most Direct Route from Mississippi to Oklahoma."

Section 4

On an annual basis, each State shall select one representative to compete in the Miss America Pageant. The representative shall have an evening gown, a bathing suit, a talent, a social concern, and a smile capable of killing small animals at close range.

Section 5

Speaking the name of the State of New Jersey shall always get a big laugh. The Constitution cannot say exactly why.

Article V

Section 1

There shall be a National Anthem containing incomprehensible words and a high note that normal humans cannot hit without risk of hernia.

Section 2

At the beginning of all major sporting events, the National Anthem shall be sung by a professional entertainer, who shall make it last as long as the musical *Cats*, and who shall get some words wrong.

Section 3

The spectators shall briefly attempt to murmur along with the professional entertainer, then go back to drinking beer.

Article VI

The Constitution shall contain a representation of giant prehistoric zucchini.

Amendments to the Constitution

Amendment I
Congress shall make no law regulating the capacity of toilets.

Amendment II
The citizens of the United States shall adopt the metric system over their dead bodies.

Amendment III
If any citizen ever has anything bad happen, for any reason, such as the citizen deliberately sticks his or her arm into a wood chipper, then that citizen shall have the right to sue everybody that his or her lawyer can think of.

Amendment IV
If a citizen is arrested, and that citizen hides his or her face from the news media, then as far as the Constitution is concerned, that citizen is *guilty*.

Amendment V
If a citizen steals a pen from the post office, boy shall *that* citizen be in trouble.

Amendment VI
The Express Lane limit shall be ten items, meaning *ten items*. Also, if a citizen takes a number at the deli counter, but does not hear the number called because he or she was off in the cereal aisle trying to decide between Lucky Charms and Cap'n Crunch, then tough noogies for that citizen.

Amendment VII

Citizens who think they have the right to arrive early at the movies and "save" seats for their friends can kiss the Constitution's rosy red behind.

Amendment VIII

And don't get the Constitution started on "light" beer.

Amendment IX

Tipping shall be 15 percent minimum for decent service. Citizens who cannot grasp this concept should not dine out.

Amendment X

Citizens shall have the right to demand salad dressing on the side. But the Constitution would like to know: *Why?*

Amendment XI

Citizens talking loudly into cellular phones shall be aware that all the other citizens hate them.

Amendment XII

Citizens under the age of twenty-one shall not be permitted to purchase intoxicating beverages without showing some form of fake ID.

Amendment XIII

If a citizen wishes to drive a "sport utility" vehicle with the same weight, fuel economy, and handling characteristics as the Lincoln Memorial, then nobody shall have the right to stop that citizen, because this is *America*, dammit.

Amendment XIV

In the interest of safety, the speed limit on inter-state highways shall be sixty-five miles per hour. (*Big Constitutional wink.*)

Amendment XV

Unauthorized reproduction of rental videos shall be punishable by death.

Amendment XVI

The Isley Brothers version of "Twist and Shout" is better than the Beatles version. There shall be no argument about this.

Amendment XVII

Every citizen, including those in comas, shall receive a minimum of one phone call per day from a very persistent stranger determined to save the citizen money on his or her long-distance bill.

Amendment XVIII

If a citizen's football team is winning a play-off game, and the team goes into the so-called prevent defense, thereby allowing the opposing team to score faster than Brad Pitt in a women's prison, then the citizen shall have the right to shoot his TV screen with a firearm that he shall have the right to keep and bear in case we ever need a well-regulated militia.

Amendment XIX

If a citizen has an appointment to see a doctor, and the citizen has to wait for more than one hour, then the citizen shall have the right to give the doctor a shot.

CHAPTER THREE

Our Government Today (or)

Protecting You from Misleadingly Named Dried Fruit

WHEN THE UNITED STATES GOVERNMENT was created in the preceding chapter, there was frankly not
much to it:

- What we now know as "Congress" consisted of a
  small group of men who met outdoors and voted by
  burping and frequently had to adjourn because of
  bears.
- The Supreme Court had only one wig, which the
  members would pass around so that whoever was
  talking could wear it.
- What we now know as the "Lincoln Memorial" was
  only four feet tall and had no beard.
- Strom Thurmond's hair was its original color.[1]

[1] Green.

The first "executive branch" consisted of the President (George Washington); the First Lady (Dolley Madison); and the Vice President (*note to editor: I will look up this person's name before the book is published*). There were only three cabinet posts: the Secretary of the Treasury, who carried the entire treasury on his person; the Secretary of War, who was responsible for making sure that both federal cannons were pointed at England; and the Secretary of Holding the President's Horse.

So our federal government had modest beginnings. It was like the lowly acorn, which starts out small and powerless, living in constant terror of squirrels. But if that lowly acorn finds itself on fertile ground and catches some lucky breaks, over the course of time it will grow and grow and grow, until finally it becomes a gigantic, powerful mutant acorn with huge, aggressive roots that can turn your septic system into a nightmare.

A similar thing happened with our government, as we can see by the chart on the next page, which represents the growth in federal spending, adjusted for inflation.

How did the government get so big? By responding to the needs of the citizens. For example, back in 1862, most Americans lived on farms. So in an effort to meet the farmers' needs, and to make sure the nation would have an adequate food supply, the government created a Department of Agriculture. Over the years, as the number of farmers grew, the Department of Agriculture, continuing to meet their needs, grew right along with them.

Then, as the nation became more urban and industrialized, and American agriculture became big business, capable of producing way more food than Americans can possibly consume, the number of actual farmers

Growth of the Federal Government
(Source: Alan Greenspan)

began to decline, and after a while dropped drastically. Today, farm families make up less than 2 percent of the American population. As a result, the Department of Agriculture has been gradually reduced in size, and today it is a minor government agency with a small budget.

It goes without saying that if you believed the previous sentence, your brain is the size of an olive pit. The Department of Agriculture is of course enormous. It spends more than $50 billion a year. *Fifty billion dollars.* That means that if we wanted, instead of having a Department of Agriculture, we could just pick out the fifty thousand poorest American farm families every year, and give every single one of them $1 million, and they could all retire to Vegas and never have to encounter a heifer again.

But of course we won't do that, because then we would not have a Department of Agriculture, which performs many vital functions, such as providing jobs for a huge number of federal employees. To quote from an official publication, Agriculture is "the third-largest civilian Department of the U.S. Government, overseeing a variety of agencies, Government corporations, and other entities that employ more than 100,000 people at over 15,000 locations in all 50 States and 80 countries."

What are all these people doing? To pick just one example, they are keeping an eye on the world oilseeds[2] market. The folks responsible for this particular agricultural angle work for the Oilseeds and Products Group, which—along with the Cotton Group, the Tobacco Group, and the Planting Seeds Group—make up

[2]Never mind what oilseeds are. It doesn't matter.

the Cotton, Oilseeds, Tobacco, and Seeds Division; which—along with the AgExport Services Division; the Dairy, Livestock, and Poultry Division; the Forest and Fishery Products Division; the Horticultural and Tropical Products Division; and the Production Estimates and Crop Assessment Division—make up the Commodity and Market Programs of Foreign Agricultural Services; which—along with the Farm Service Agency, the Risk Management Agency, and the Commodity Credit Corporation—make up the Farm and Foreign Agricultural Services; which—along with Rural Development; Food, Nutrition, and Consumer Services; Food Safety; Natural Resources and Environment; Research, Education, and Economics; and Marketing and Regulatory Programs—make up the seven "mission areas" of what is described in official government publications, with a straight typeface, as the "streamlined" Department of Agriculture.

I realize this is all pretty difficult for a normal civilian taxpayer brain to comprehend. Perhaps it will be simpler if we view this information in graphical form:

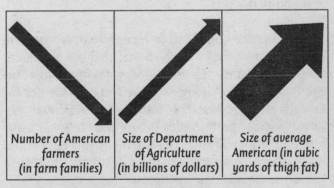

| Number of American farmers (in farm families) | Size of Department of Agriculture (in billions of dollars) | Size of average American (in cubic yards of thigh fat) |

Agriculture and the Federal Government

I don't mean to single out agriculture. Another need that the American people have is education, and to meet that need, the federal government has provided a Department of Education, which spends around $40 billion a year and employs thousands of workers, who improve the quality of education via such tactics as writing Mission Statements. A Mission Statement is a dense slab of words that a large organization produces when it needs to establish that its workers are not just sitting around downloading Internet porn. For example, what follows is an actual quotation from a Department of Education Mission Statement (CAUTION! *Do not read if you are operating heavy machinery!*):

> The mission of this Institute is to provide national leadership and support to develop and disseminate information that helps guide the design and implementation of effective governance strategies, coherent policy formation, reasonable management decisions, and equitable finance allocations that will support high levels of learning by all students.

That, in case you failed to recognize it, is from the Mission Statement for the National Institute on Educational Governance, Finance, Policymaking, and Management, which—along with the National Center for Education Statistics; the National Educational Research Policy and Priorities Board; the National Institute on Early Childhood Development and Education; the National Institute on the Education of At-Risk Students; the National Institute on Postsecondary Education, Libraries, and Lifelong Learning; the National

Institute on Student Achievement, Curriculum, and Assessment; the National Library of Education; the National Research and Development Centers; and the Office of Reform Assistance and Dissemination—make up the Office of Educational Research and Improvement, which—along with the Office of Bilingual Education and Minority Languages Affairs; the Office for Civil Rights; the Office of Elementary and Secondary Education; the Office of Postsecondary Education; the Office of Special Educational and Rehabilitative Services; the Offices of Student Financial Assistance Programs; and the Office of Vocational and Adult Education—makes up the program offices (just the *program* offices, mind you) of the Department of Education.

Again, this is pretty complex stuff for the civilian mind, so here's a statistical chart to help you understand it:

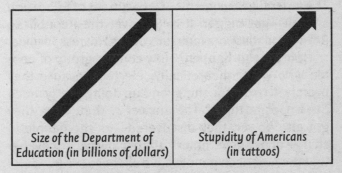

Size of the Department of   Stupidity of Americans
Education (in billions of dollars)   (in tattoos)

Education and the Federal Government

The point is that, whatever the needs of the public are, the government responds to those needs by getting larger. It makes no difference who's running the government. For example, in 1994 we had the

Republican Revolution, in which Congress was taken
over by conservative, anti–Big Government Republicans led by a fervently spherical Georgia congressperson named Newt Gingrich.

These people *hated* Big Government. They talked
as though they were going to implement mass exe-
cutions of federal employees. The Republicans were
definitely going to Cut Federal Spending and Fight
Government Waste and Get Rid of Bloated, Unnecessary Bureaucracies. Especially the Department of
Education! That money pit was *outta* here!

Bear in mind that these people were not just a
bunch of random blowhards. They were a bunch of
blowhards who were *in control of the United States Congress.* If *anybody* could reduce the size of the federal
government, it would, theoretically, be these people.

And what happened? You know what happened.
The federal government—Department of Education
and all—got bigger. It rolled over the Republican
Revolution the way a tank rolls over a Hostess Twinkie.

How did this happen? How could a group of people who were, theoretically, elected because they
promised to do one thing, end up doing pretty much
the opposite thing? The answer is that, once they
got into power, they discovered—as the people in
charge of our government almost always discover—
that the American people have all these *needs.*

To pick just one of many examples: In 1998, when
Congress was deciding what the American people
needed in the way of national defense, it decided
to buy $400 million's worth of C-130 cargo planes
for the military. The thing was, the actual military, in
the form of the Pentagon, never asked for these

planes, and in fact had stated explicitly that it did not want them. But the cost-cutting, waste-fighting, Republican-controlled Congress said: Who are *you* to decide you don't want these planes? You do *too* want these planes, dammit! In fact, since 1978, Congress has ordered the Pentagon to buy *hundreds* of C-130 planes that the Pentagon didn't want. Congress does this for two reasons:

1. The planes are made at a Lockheed-Martin plant in Georgia that has traditionally had powerful advocates in Congress, such as (to pick a name at random) Newt Gingrich.
2. After the planes are built, they are usually sent to Air National Guard and Air Force Reserve bases in areas such as Harrisburg, Pennsylvania, represented by influential congresspersons. The function of these planes is to fly around and make the bases look busy, so that the congresspersons can claim the bases are vital to national security, when in fact in many cases the Pentagon would like to shut them down, based on the growing belief in the military intelligence community that the Russians do not have any immediate designs on Harrisburg.

In other words, influential members of Congress have decided that the American people need to buy military planes that the military leaders don't want, which are used to justify the existence of military bases that the military leaders also don't want, so that large quantities of money will flow into the districts of these influential members of Congress, so that they can get reelected and continue to decide what the American people need. From a defense standpoint, it would make just about as much sense to stop building new C-130s, and simply have the old C-130s fly over Marietta and Harrisburg and drop hundred-dollar bills. But of course this is unacceptable: You run the risk that the wind would blow some of the money into the wrong congressperson's district.

One more example: Senate Majority Leader Trent Lott, who presents himself as a fiscal conservative and who is from Pascagoula, Mississippi, decided that the U.S. Navy needed a helicopter assault ship, and that this ship would be built in, well, Pascagoula, Mississippi. The Navy had not asked for this ship, but it was pretty much ordered to come up with an estimate of the amount of money that would be required to get this project started. The Navy said $295 million.

Now $295 million probably sounds like a lot of money to a lowly wormlike taxpayer such as you, but it is peanuts to a Senate Majority Leader who is in tune with the defense needs of the American people. So a member of Senator Lott's staff fired off a fax to a Navy admiral stating that $295 million was, quote, "the wrong answer." The fax informed the admiral that Senator Lott was looking for a number more in the range of "$375 to $500 million." Senator Lott got $375 million to start work on the ship, which ultimately will cost taxpayers, in round figures, $1.5 billion.

Another way of looking at this is that if you added up all the taxes you will pay in your entire life, and all the taxes everybody in your family will pay, and all the taxes that everybody you know will ever pay—all that money that all of you just gave to the government—you'd still be *way* more than $1 billion short of what Senator Lott believes the American people need to pay for a U.S. Navy ship that the U.S. Navy did not ask for. (Just in case you're wondering if Senator Lott has the necessary background to be giving orders to the U.S. Navy about what ships it needs, consider this: Back in the sixties, when many young men of college age were avoiding military service, Trent Lott served, with distinction, as a cheerleader at Ole Mississippi.)

I realize that I've been singling out Republicans here. This is only because the Republicans are usually the ones who promise to Do Something about Big Government. The Democrats don't even pretend they're going to do that: They're *crazy* for Big Government. Whereas the Republicans at least *talk* about cutting spending and taxes, this concept never seems to cross the minds of the Democrats. Even during times of huge federal surpluses, when we taxpayers are shipping excess money to Washington by the ton, the Democrats frankly cannot imagine giving any of it back to us; they would infinitely rather invent new programs that they feel we need. When there's a debate between two Democratic candidates, it sounds like this:

FIRST DEMOCRAT: I would guarantee affordable medical care for every American!

SECOND DEMOCRAT: Well, I would guarantee *free* medical care for every American!

FIRST DEMOCRAT: Oh yeah? Well I would guarantee free medical care for everybody in the United States *and their pets!*

SECOND DEMOCRAT: Oh *yeah*? Well I would also guar-
    antee free medical care for everybody in Mexico
    and Canada!

FIRST DEMOCRAT: Oh YEAH? Well I would guarantee
    free medical care *even for people who didn't need*
    it! I would have squads of armed federal em-
    ployees burst into healthy people's homes and
    forcibly remove their spleens!

SECOND DEMOCRAT: OH YEAH?! Well, I would dig up
    dead people and give them . . .

So both parties are responsible for the growth of
government. Perhaps you think that the problem is
that we elect the wrong kind of people to Congress.
Perhaps you also think that if *you*—a regular taxpayer, a commonsense kind of person—were in
Congress, *you* would do something about government spending. Please do not think I am being rude
when I respond by making a derisive farting noise
with my mouth.

First of all, you *can't* get elected to Congress, because under our political system, pretty much the
only way to get elected to Congress is to raise a
bunch of campaign money, and pretty much the
only way to do *that* is to already be a member of
Congress. But let's say a miracle occurs. Let's say the
incumbent congressperson you run against is photo-
graphed naked in a motel room with a Shetland pony
who is not his wife, and you actually get elected.

So you go to Washington, where your plan is to
fight for the regular taxpayer. Except guess what?
Once you're in Washington, *you never see any regular taxpayers.* They're all back home working so they

can pay their taxes. The people who come around to see you in Washington are members of organized groups who are seeking Access to the Political Process, by which I mean: Money. The basic deal is, if you'll give them access, they'll give you support, by which I also mean: Money.

So you'll find that you spend most of your time sitting in your office listening to people from organizations with names like the Association of Organic Weasel Breeders, who tell you, in mind-numbing detail, how important the organic weasel-breeding industry is to the economic health of the nation in general and your district in particular. They'll show you heartrending pictures of sad-looking out-of-work weasel breeders and their hungry, lice-ridden children. They'll explain how this once-thriving industry, and the cherished way of life it represents, will be destroyed unless the government takes action against the giant Taiwanese weasel ranches, or the Microsoft Corporation's ruthless program to develop a virtual weasel,[3] or whatever bee they happen to have in their special-interest bonnet. They will make it clear that, as far as they are concerned, this is the most important issue facing the planet today.

Finally, just to get rid of them, you'll promise to see if you can do something. The instant they leave your office, they're replaced by a group of representatives of the United Brotherhood of Sprocket Polishers, who will back you up to a wall (they are large people) and ask you if you have *any idea* how

[3]"Virtual Weasel" would be a good name for a rock band.

many union sprocket polishers live in your district,[4] and what percentage of the sprockets sold in America today is being polished in foreign sweatshops. And when they finally leave, you're facing the lobbyists for the Federation of Manufacturers of Those Rubber Bands That Hold Lobster Claws Shut in Restaurant Tanks, who will persuasively make the case that if you won't do anything for their troubled industry and its many threatened employees in your district, you are no better than the cowards who stood by and did nothing when Hitler took over Czechoslovakia.

And so it goes, day after brain-deadening day. Every time you turn around, you get hammered on by people who want you to do something for them, and that something *never* involves saving the taxpayers money. You start looking around at the other congresspersons, who are all fighting for the needs of *their* special interests, and you say to yourself, "Hey, if the government is going to help the oilseeds growers, what's wrong with doing a little something for the sprocket polishers?" And so you find a way to help them out, maybe get them a couple million dollars' worth of access, which you rationalize by telling yourself that a couple million dollars is *nothing* in Washington. The federal government spends that kind of money on dental floss. But to the sprocket polishers, you are a *hero*. They will go to the mattresses to get you reelected, so you can keep meeting their needs.

After a while you learn that it is generally a bad

---

[4]They have bumper stickers that proclaim: I'M A UNION SPROCKET POLISHER—AND I VOTE!

idea, as a member of Congress, to vote against spending money on *anything*. If you do, the taxpayers whose money you're trying to save won't know about it, but whatever interest group you voted against will be on you like army ants. If you vote to cut the Department of Agriculture, farmers will hate you. If you vote to cut the Department of Education, the teachers' unions hate you. If you dared to suggest that maybe we don't need to pay for the prescription drugs of wealthy retirees who own, say, more than three yachts, members of the American Association of Retired People will beat you senseless with handicapped-parking placards.

And so before long you're just like everybody else in Congress, handing out access, taking in support, and helping to pass budgets that, no matter what, get bigger every year. Sure, you still call yourself a fiscal conservative opposed to Big Government, but that doesn't mean you have no heart! That doesn't mean you want your children to grow up in a country that is too callous to provide subsidies for needy weasel breeders!

And that's basically why the federal government grows. Nothing can stop it, except maybe (not that I am advocating this) a direct asteroid hit on the Capitol Building. And even that probably wouldn't work. Even if the entire District of Columbia were transformed into a gigantic two-mile-deep hole, taxpayers would be required to stand around the edge and throw money into the smoking cavity.

So there is nothing that anybody can do to prevent the federal government from growing and bloating and spending unfathomable amounts of money on things that most regular taxpayers, if anybody ever asked them, would say they do not want.

But is there not another side to this coin? Doesn't the government also give us many benefits?

It most surely does. And I am not just talking about obvious things such as social security, a wondrously generous program under which, after we spend our entire working lives sending money to the government, we retire, and the government—this is such a deal—*starts sending money back.* No, I'm talking about federal benefits that most of us are not aware of and could not even imagine without a major disruption of brain tissue.

For example: Back in 1999, the California Prune Board, which is probably the number one[5] prune-related organization in the United States, decided that it wanted to call prunes "dried plums." This was because marketing research has shown that "dried plums" has more appeal than "prunes" to American consumers.

Before I proceed, let me clarify one point: Prunes are, in fact, dried plums. I checked this out in the dictionary, as well as on the official web site of the California Prune Board, www.prunes.org.[6] This site has a lot of interesting prune facts and a section called "Prune History," where we learn that prunes originated in the Caucasus Mountains and eventually made their way to the Balkans, "where they have

[5]This is not a play on words.
[6]Another excellent prune-related web site is Dole Food's www.dole5aday.com, where you can actually hear a spoken message from Perry Prunes.

thrived ever since."⁷ Prunes were introduced to North America in 1856 by a Frenchman named Louis Pellier, who had come to California in search of gold but apparently did not find any, so he decided— as so many dreamers do when their dreams are dashed—to grow prunes. The result is the world-famous California French prune, which according to the Prune Board is prized for, among other things, its "smooth small pits."

So anyway, you might think that since prunes are in fact dried plums, the Prune Board could just go ahead and call them that, but of course you would be wrong. The Prune Board needed to ask the permission of the Office of Food Labeling, which—along with the Office of Cosmetics and Colors, the Office of Premarket Approval, the Office of Plant and Dairy Foods and Beverages, the Office of Seafood, the Office of Special Nutritionals, the Office of Special Research Skills, the Office of Field Programs, and the Office of Scientific Analysis and Support—makes up the Center for Food Safety and Applied Nutrition, which—along with the Office of Regulatory Affairs, the National Center for Toxicological Research, the Center for Biologics Evaluation and Research, the Center for Drug Evaluation and Research, the Center for Devices and Radiological Health, and the Center for Veterinary Medicine—makes up the Food and Drug Administration, which—together with the Administration for Children and Families, the Administration on Aging, the Agency for Health Care Policy

⁷"The Thriving Balkan Prunes" would also be a good name for a rock band.

and Research, the Agency for Toxic Substances and Disease Registry, the Centers for Disease Control and Prevention, the Health Care Financing Administration, the Health Resources and Services Administration, the Indian Health Service, the National Institutes of Health, the Program Support Center, and the Substance Abuse and Mental Health Services Administration—makes up the Department of Health and Human Services.

So when the request came in—and in case you have forgotten what we're talking about, we're talking about the request of the California Prune Board to be allowed to call prunes, which are dried plums, "dried plums"—the Food and Drug Administration immediately did: Nothing. Several months went by with no response (maybe everybody was busy writing Mission Statements). So both of California's U.S. senators wrote to the Food and Drug Administration asking what the deal was. Six more months passed, and then FDA associate commissioner Melinda K. Plaisier responded with a letter stating that "We are concerned that calling prunes by another name could be misleading to the consumer." Plaisier said the FDA wanted more information,[8] including "the effect [on FDA regulations] of renaming prunes," "international aspects of changing the name," "results of consumer research including United States and foreign studies," "other labeling

_____

[8]I got this information from Al Kamen's highly informative and entertaining *Washington Post* column "In the Loop," which, if you are a taxpayer, can simultaneously make you laugh *and* want to kill yourself.

options and why they would be ineffective," information on why "the prune is marketed more successfully in Europe than in the United States," and "a plan of action for educating consumers about the name change and information about plums and prunes that is available on Web sites."

Early in 2000 I spoke with the head man at the Prune Board, Rich Peterson, about this issue. He told me he was "cautiously optimistic" that the FDA would eventually allow the industry to call prunes "dried plums." He also said the public had been supportive.

"People are somewhat incredulous that the FDA would not allow us to say that prunes are dried plums," he said.

And of course there you have exactly the reason why this kind of decision is not left up to the public. The public is, frankly, not capable of comprehending the numerous implications—the *international* implications—of the prunes versus dried plums issue, any more than the public understands the helicopter assault ship issue, or the oilseeds issue,[9] or the almost infinite number of other issues that Congress and the president and the hundreds of federal agencies with their hundreds of thousands of employees are constantly dealing with on our behalf, demanding nothing from us in return except that we send them large chunks of our incomes and inheritances.

So to summarize this chapter: The federal government has become gigantic, unbelievably expensive, insanely complicated, and absurdly bossy. Yet often this same government is sincerely trying, in

[9] I'm assuming that there is an oilseeds issue.

its clumsy federal way, to do the right thing, to help us, much as King Kong sincerely believed he was helping Fay Wray when he carried her against her will up the Empire State Building.

And so we must now ask ourselves: Can this system be fixed? Can we, the people, by taking an active political role and *demanding* change, bring about meaningful reform of the federal government—reform that would retain the positive elements, and at the same time eliminate the waste, the fraud, the abuse, the stupidity? That is the question that I intend to answer in this book. In fact, I'll answer it right now: No, we can't.

So instead, we should learn to view the federal government as *entertainment*—a comedy extravaganza, featuring the kind of madcap craziness and wacky hijinks that you can get only when you give nearly $2 trillion a year to an organization with the proven financial management expertise of a tub of bait. This book will be a celebration of that entertainment. So sit back, grab a dried plum, and enjoy it. Hey, you paid for it.[10]

---

[10]I mean you paid for the government. I'm *hoping* you didn't pay for this book.

CHAPTER FOUR

Touring Washington, D.C. (or)

The Many Wonders of Wing Tip World

IF YOU'RE LIKE MILLIONS OF AMERICANS, your first, and maybe only, visit to Washington, D.C., was on a class trip. I'm talking about the kind of trip for which your class raised money by coercing your relatives and neighbors to buy something utterly useless, such as a car wash that actually left the victim's car dirtier, or Christmas cards that you didn't get around to delivering until Ground-hog Day.

Hassling innocent people for class-trip money is a cherished American student tradition. The trip to Washington is considered to be the ultimate educational event—a chance for young people to visit their nation's capital and see, in person, how far they can stick their tongues into one another's mouths. Because heavy petting in the back of the bus is a *major* element of every class trip. I don't care if it's the senior class of the Extremely Christian Academy for Unattractive Young People Wearing Chastity Belts; I don't care if every single chaperone holds the rank of ayatollah or higher. Once those buses get rolling, there is *going* to be some saliva exchanged.

I'm not saying that sex is the only thing that happens on class trips. As a student visiting the capital, you also learn many important educational lessons, such as:

1. How to moon pedestrians from a moving bus.

2. How to stand in your hotel doorway, teetering back and forth and reeking of beer, and attempt to convince the physical education teacher, Mr. Bomperman—who is wearing, on his left shoulder, a semidigested piece of the pizza you had for dinner—that it may have been a student who *looked* exactly like you, but it was not, in fact, you, who barfed on him out the hotel window.

3. How important it is—you realize this as the U.S. Capitol police are stripping you for a cavity search—to believe the signs stating that bomb threats, even *highly amusing* bomb threats, will be taken seriously.

Yes, there is a lot to learn on a class trip to Washington, D.C., which is why most students never actually see much of Washington, D.C. If you go to the U.S. Capitol Building in the spring, which is the height of class-trip season, you'll see school groups everywhere, and they all look pretty much the same: A bunch of people forming a random clot in some random corridor in front of some random statue, while a random tour guide informs them of some random historical fact, such as that it was on this exact spot 154 years ago that the historic Alfalfa Crisis began when Senator Barton A. Mousewrangler, Jr., of Tennessee blew his nose on the historic Fodder Reserve Act of 1827.

Standing close to the guide, listening with interest, is a cluster of maybe eight people, consisting of the chaperones and a couple of kiss-ass, goody-two-shoes students, the kind who join the Future Wing Tips of Tomorrow and get admitted to Harvard in ninth grade. But outside of this attentive cluster, the rest of the students are snoozing, gossiping, giggling, groping one another, and seeing how far the sound of a human fart will carry in a historic federal corridor.[1]

The odds are that, on your class trip, you were one of these outlying students. So in this chapter, we're going to fill this gap in your education. You're going to take a "virtual tour" of the amazing city of Washington, D.C., the only city in the nation where the phrase "federal worker" is not automatically considered funny. Turn the page, and we'll start with:

---

[1] The record is 2,038 yards, set by Senator Strom Thurmond in 1874.

The History of Washington, D.C.

In the early years, the United States did not have a permanent capital, forcing Congress to meet, at various times, in Philadelphia, New York, Richmond, Mexico City, and Vegas. All this moving around was time-consuming and laborious, because some parts of the federal government, particularly the Lincoln Memorial, were extremely heavy.

So in 1790 Congress decided to create a permanent capital by taking a piece of land from Virginia, a piece of land from Maryland, and a piece of land from Vermont that was hauled in at great expense. Congress chose this location for four reasons:

1. It was near Chevy Chase.
2. It was shaped pretty much like a square.
3. It was located on the Potomac River, which guaranteed that the capital would have an abundant natural supply of humidity.
4. It had already been settled by a small but hardy population of lobbyists, who produced nothing but had been able to survive for decades in the harsh wilderness by taking one another to lunch.

The new capital was named after the first American president, George Washington, or "D.C." for short. The plan for the city was created by a French architect named Pierre L'Enfant,[2] who had already gained a considerable reputation for designing the Eiffel Tower.

[2] Literally, "Ivan the Terrible."

L'Enfant envisioned a city with streets that formed a logical, easy-to-understand grid pattern. But then he drank two quarts of corn liquor and laid out the present-day Washington, which has streets running in totally random directions, then coming together in giant inscrutable spiderweb-like circles constructed around statues of famous dead generals. There were so many of these circles that L'Enfant eventually had to execute some famous living generals to meet the demand. That's the kind of stickler he was.[3]

In 1800 the federal government officially moved to Washington. Early life in the capital was hard. Plastic had not been invented yet, so federal employees had to wear cast-iron ID badges weighing as much as thirty pounds. The only mass transit available was a primitive subway system consisting of one stop, a 450-foot-deep hole near what is now DuPont Circle. Every morning commuters would climb laboriously to the bottom, get their parchment fare cards stamped, climb laboriously back out, then trudge home, exhausted.

The streets of Washington were full of potholes, which today are painstakingly maintained in their original condition by the Department of Historic Pothole Preservation. (Another road-related tradition that has continued into modern times is that the entire city shuts down if it snows, or it looks like it might snow, or anybody named "Snow" is visiting the area.)

The pace of life in Washington picked up when the British invaded in 1814, as part of the War of 1812, which was running late because of scheduling

[3]Hence the term "French stickler."

problems. British troops burned down the White House, but not before First Lady Dolley Madison carried off and hid a portrait of George Washington and some billing records from the Rose Law Firm of Little Rock, Arkansas, which were not found for 184 years. British troops also burned down a number of other buildings housing critical government agencies, including the Mule Standards Administration, the Saltpeter Reserve Board, and the Department of Tallow and Suet Affairs.

This was a devastating setback, but over the next ten years, the proud and plucky citizens of Washington painstakingly rebuilt their city, at which point the British troops, who had been standing around watching, burned everything down again. Fed up, the federal government decreed that henceforth all important government buildings would be constructed of stone, which cannot be set on fire, although visiting taxpayers routinely try.

The Civil War (1861–present) posed the next big threat for Washington. Confederate troops massed within sight of the Capitol, although they were unable to enter the city because all the hotels were fully booked with class trips. On April 14, 1865, one of Washington's, and the nation's, greatest tragedies occurred in Ford's Theatre, where Abraham Lincoln, attending a performance of *Cats*, was assassinated by actor John Wilkes Booth, who then leaped onto the stage and broke his leg. As the nation grieved, an outraged Congress met in emergency session and created the Occupational Safety and Health Administration (OSHA), to ensure that nothing like this would ever happen again.

Over the next few decades, as the United States expanded, the city of Washington also grew, because the federal government hired thousands of additional federal employees to carry out the important federal work that needed to be done at that time on the federal level. During this era the city was governed by officials who were appointed by Congress; the residents of Washington were not allowed to vote for their own leaders, or for the president. (Ironically, they *were* allowed to vote for members of the Italian parliament.) Gradually the issue of self-government became a thorn in the side that stuck in the city's craw, forming a bone of contention that would eventually stick out like a sore thumb.

Fortunately, before the metaphors could get completely out of hand, World War I[4] broke out, and with the future of democracy hanging in the balance, Washingtonians set aside their personal concerns and buckled down to the task of developing detailed written specifications for soldier hats.[5] During this era the automobile replaced the horse as the primary mode of transportation in Washington; Congress, facing the problem of what to do with thousands of government-owned horses, created the federal school-lunch program, which remains just as popular with youngsters today as it ever was.

After the war, Prohibition was passed, and with liquor no longer legally available the nation plunged headlong into the Great Depression. President Franklin "D" Roosevelt responded by getting Congress to

[4]Or, as it was known in those days, "The War Before World War II."
[5]This project was completed in 1987.

create the WPA, the NRA, the PWA, and the NLRB; as a result, the federal government hired tens of thousands of new employees to try to figure out what these initials stood for. In 1932, some twenty-five thousand poor veterans, called "Bonus Marchers," descended on Washington and, desperate for a place to sleep, formed the Department of Commerce, which is still there today, although nobody knows why.

World War II, as its name suggests, plunged the world into a war for the second time, and the federal government responded by going on a war footing, which meant hiring tens of thousands more employees to perform urgent combat-related typing (although we should not forget that, as the war progressed, many of these employees were also called upon to file). During this era many new office buildings were hastily erected in Washington, but the authorities never found out who was responsible.

After the war, the nation settled down to a period of relative tranquillity, forcing the federal government to make the transition to a relative tranquillity footing, which required the hiring of tens of thousands more employees. By now, all of these worker influxes had dramatically transformed Washington from a boring, stodgy, uncultured city into a boring, stodgy, uncultured city that was more densely populated.

But all that was to change radically as the complacent fifties gave way to the idealistic sixties, and in 1963 President John F. Kennedy electrified the nation with his pledge that, by the end of the decade, no matter how many billions of dollars it cost, Man would be able to travel all the way around Washington by car. This led to the construction of the

Beltway, and although Kennedy, tragically, did not live to see it, those of us who were alive at the time will never forget where we were on August 17, 1964, when America held its breath as a new national hero, Parnell M. Smeedle, an accountant from Silver Spring, Maryland, climbed into his Plymouth Valiant and successfully completed the first solo orbit of the District, completing the trip in eight hours, seventeen minutes, and thirty-six seconds—a record that has never been broken.

In the same spirit of sixties "can-do" optimism, Kennedy's successor, Lyndon Johnson, soon created the "Great Society"—a wide-ranging group of programs with the breathtakingly ambitious goal of eliminating poverty and racism, for once and for all, by hiring tens of thousands more federal employees.

But the sixties were not all fun and games for Washington. The city became the site of many mass protests, some of which were marred by violent clashes between protesters and the National Park Service over the size of the crowd estimates. But the low point came in 1967, when the tinderbox of urban unrest reached the boiling point. In a tragedy from which it would take Washington decades to fully recover, a large area of the downtown business district was burned by a rampaging mob of elderly British troops.

But Washington—which proudly calls itself "The City Too Busy Holding Hearings to Think of What to Call Itself"—recovered and rebuilt, mostly in Maryland and Virginia. The downtown area continued to decay, and by the seventies Washington was gripped by a crime wave, much of which was ultimately traced to a vicious, highly organized urban gang calling itself "The Committee to Reelect the President." In outraged response, the American voters demanded meaningful political reform, which need-less to say required the hiring of tens of thousands more federal employees.

In 1974 Congress finally gave Washington resi-dents the right to elect their own leaders, and in 1978 they elected, as their mayor, Marion "Party Time" Barry, who improved living conditions in Washing-ton by giving a city job to pretty much every adult resident who was not either a federal employee or dead.[6] This made Barry very popular, and thus he was ultimately able to recover from the scandal that erupted in 1990 when FBI agents videotaped him smoking crack in a hotel room with British troops who were not his wife. After serving time in prison, a totally rehabilitated, morally reborn Marion Barry came back in 1994 to be reelected[7] mayor after cam-paigning on the inspirational slogan: "Next Time, He'll Post a Lookout."

Yes, Washington has had its troubles. But it has emerged from those troubles to become one of the most vibrant and cosmopolitan cities in the entire southern Maryland area; a city where, as a visitor, you experience the thrill of knowing that you are at the epi-center of federal power, and at any moment you, an or-dinary citizen, could turn a corner and find yourself

[6] Not that these two categories are mutually exclusive.
[7] I am not making this up: In its report on this mayoral election, the September 15, 1994, *Miami Herald* quoted a Washington resi-dent who voted for Barry as saying: "Do you know how many drug addicts there are in D.C.? They all voted this time."

bumping into the Deputy Administrative Assistant to the Assistant Executive Deputy Associate Administrator to the Acting Interim Executive Undersecretary for Coordination of Interstate Urban Fish Hatchery Affairs, or one of his top aides!

But even if you don't encounter any major Washington celebrities, you are bound to have a swell time because there are so many large and historic stone things to see and do in Washington, after waiting in line. So let's get started on our virtual tour! We'll start by taking you to the very "heart of the action," which of course is:

Capitol Hill

The huge gleaming white dome of the U.S. Capitol is one of the dominant visual elements of Washington, looming up over the center of the city like—to quote the dead poet Walt Whitman—"some kind of great big visual element." It is here that the nation's laws are hammered out by the two bodies that, together, form the legislative branch of our government: (1) Lobbyists, and (2) Lobbyists for the Other Side.

Also performing an important legislative function—namely, reading speeches written by other people—are members of the U.S. Senate and House of Representatives, who can often be seen striding briskly through the corridors of the Capitol, trailed by aides holding briefcases and talking into cell phones. Sometimes the congresspersons are on their way to important hearings. Sometimes they're on their way to the bathroom. Sometimes they have no destination at all: They're just striding around in an important manner, which is a popular leisure activity on Capitol Hill. A congressperson will be sitting in his office, bored, and suddenly he'll say to his aides: "Grab your phones! It's time to stride!"

And off they'll go, sometimes striding for miles before their batteries run out. Occasionally two striding-congressperson formations will simultaneously reach a blind corner from opposite directions and collide at high speeds, sending briefcases and wing tips flying everywhere. This is why your newer congresspersons are equipped with air bags.

A Brief History of the Capitol Building

The cornerstone of the U.S. Capitol was laid in 1793 by George Washington on a site carefully selected by surveyors. Unfortunately, the cornerstone was stolen that night and abandoned in a bad neighborhood, so that's where the Capitol ended up being built.

By 1800 construction of the Capitol was complete, and the dome immediately began filling with rainwater, because the builders, having read the plans incorrectly, had constructed it upside down. After everybody enjoyed a hearty laugh and the contractor was executed, workers knocked the Capitol down and started over, completing the rebuilding in 1814, when President James Polk Madison, in a formal ceremony attended by leaders of both the House and Senate, set the new Capitol on fire, thus depriving British troops of the pleasure.

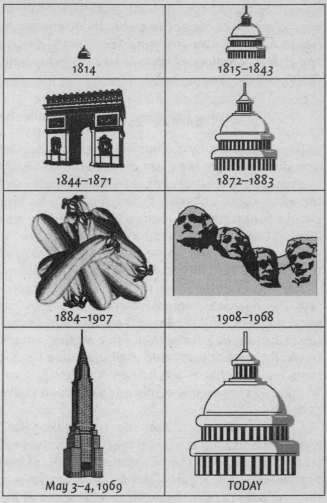

1814

1815–1843

1844–1871

1872–1883

1884–1907

1908–1968

May 3–4, 1969

TODAY

Architectural Development of the U.S. Capitol
(Source: American Association of Architectural Historians on Crack)

The Capitol was again rebuilt, and over the following 150 years it continued to be expanded and modified to meet the ever-changing needs of the Senate and House of Representatives, as we see in the renderings on the previous page.

Touring the Capitol

The place to start your tour is in the **Rotunda,** the area directly under the giant **dome,** which is nearly 150 years old and weighs nine million pounds, and therefore could collapse at any moment. So you should sprint across this area while glancing upward at the giant **fresco** painted in 1865 by an important **Italian artist** whose name we need to look up before we send this manuscript to the **publisher.**

The figures in the inner ring of the fresco represent the **thirteen original colonies;** those in the outer ring represent the **Seven Dwarfs.** Near the very top of the Rotunda can be seen some **writing,** which, tragically, was not translated until 1943, when historians realized that it was Italian for: "Help, I am trapped up here on this scaffold and will soon starve to death."

To the south of the Rotunda is **Statuary Hall,** which contains statues representing two distinguished citizens from each of the fifty states. (Arkansas is represented by a nice pair of **garden gnomes.**) Along the **corridors** to both the north and the south of the Rotunda are many historic and artistic **paintings, statues, frescoes,** and **friezes** that pretty soon will bore the living **shit** out of you. So you should go visit the **House** and **Senate chambers,** where you can see the numerous **seats** where your elected representatives would be sitting if they were there, which they almost never are, because they're out striding through corridors or meeting with people who might give them **money.**

The best place to see actual legislators is in the **House of Representatives,** during the time set aside for "one-minute" speeches. These are the little speeches that congresspersons make, with great drama and passion, to a room that is basically empty except for the C-SPAN camera, which broadcasts the House proceedings live to a nationwide audience consisting of, basically, the C-SPAN cameraman.

☞ *Digression Alert*

Because nobody is paying attention to the "one-minute" speeches, members of the House can say pretty much anything. I know this because I once wrote one of these speeches. I am not making this up. In 1995, to research a story, I spent a week working on the staff of U.S. Representative Steven C. LaTourette, a Republican from Ohio's 19th District.[8] I doubt that Representative LaTourette fully understood what he was getting into when he allowed me to join his staff. For example, he appeared somewhat disconcerted when, in an effort to drum up publicity for him, I strongly hinted to the Associated Press that Representative LaTourette was born, biologically, a woman.[9]

Fortunately, Representative LaTourette has a good

---

[8] Which, needless to say, includes Ashtabula.
[9] This is not true. To my knowledge.

sense of humor. I found this out when the House Republican leadership asked its members to give speeches opposing frivolous lawsuits. I wrote such a speech, and, to my amazement, Representative La-Tourette actually got up and delivered it on the floor of the House. Here's the complete text:

Mr. Speaker:

As a lawyer, I am the last person to suggest that everybody in my profession is a money-grubbing, scum-sucking toad. The actual figure is only about 73 percent.

Ha ha, I am of course just pulling the speaker's honorable leg. The vast majority of lawyers are responsible professionals as well as, in many ways, human beings.

But we really do need to do something about all these frivolous lawsuits. We've reached the point where a simple product such as a stepladder has to be sold with big red *warning* labels all over it, telling you not to dance on it, hold parties on it, touch electrical wires with it, hit people with it, swallow it, etc., because some idiot somewhere, sometime, actually *did* these things with a stepladder, got hurt, filed a lawsuit—and *won*.

My feeling, Mr. Speaker, is that anybody who swallows a stepladder deserves whatever he gets. And I'm sure the vast majority of the American people would agree with me. The minority would probably sue.

Not only did Representative LaTourette deliver this speech, but also the full text was printed in the

Congressional Record. Nobody better try to tell *me* this is not a great country.

☞ End of Digression Alert

While you're on Capitol Hill, you should definitely visit the office of your congressperson. All congressional offices are located near the Capitol in some **hideously ugly buildings.**

To locate your specific congressperson, go into one of these buildings and open a door at random; you should see a **receptionist.** Go up to this person and say: "Hi! I'm *(your name)* from *(your state)*. Where's my congressperson's office?" If the receptionist cannot answer, or starts asking you for obscure information such as your congressperson's name (as if you would *ever* know *that*), remind the receptionist in a firm but loud voice that you are a taxpayer, dammit, and you did not come all the way to Washington, D.C., to be treated in a snotty manner.

When you eventually locate your congressperson's office, remember that, because we live in a republic, it's really *your* office. Feel free to use the phone, rearrange the furniture, help yourself to office supplies, or leave your kids with your congressperson while you go shopping. Your congressperson is there to serve you! At least that's what he says in all those newsletters he mails to you at your expense.

Tipping: It is customary to tip your congressperson a dollar for each child you leave for more than twelve hours. If you wish your congressperson to provide an extra service, such as holding a hearing or introducing a bill, the suggested gratuity is $5,000.

Elsewhere on Capitol Hill you may visit the **Library of Congress,** which has over 100 million books, documents, and other resource materials used by Congress in preparing legislation, including every issue of *Hustler* ever published (ask for directions to the **Bob Packwood Wing**). The Library has a staff of highly trained researchers who can answer any questions you have. Like, if you have a melody stuck in your head, and it's driving you nuts because you can't think of what song it is, just hum it in the Library of Congress **Humming Room,** and the staff will shout out the title.[10] If you make arrangements in advance, you can visit the vault containing what the federal government believes to be the lyrics to **"Louie Louie."** In the basement of the Library of Congress is the **world's largest sports betting operation.**

A short distance away is the **Supreme Court Building,** which is one of the most popular tour stops in Washington. When the court is in session, the justices welcome audience participation, so don't hesitate to leap to your feet and shout "OBJECTION!" or "I CONFESS! I'M THE REAL KILLER!" Every Thursday from 7 to 11 P.M. is **Karaoke Night** at the Supreme Court.

Just a few steps from the Supreme Court is the **National Historic Museum of Office Supplies,** which houses the world's largest public collection of hand-carved whalebone staples. Don't miss *Dark Secret,*

---

[10]"Candy Man," as sung by Sammy Davis, Jr.

the award-winning documentary film that tells the riveting story of how a classified United States government project to develop a better copier toner during the sixties ultimately turned the tide in the Cold War.

The Mall

No trip to Washington is complete without a visit to the **Mall.** I am not speaking figuratively, here: If you try to leave the city without visiting the Mall, soldiers will stop you at the border. That's how mandatory this visit is.

You will begin your tour by going to the **Smithsonian Institution,** which is sometimes called the "Nation's Attic" because it contains a huge quantity of **dead insects.** It also houses, in various buildings around the Mall, a vast collection of priceless national memorabilia, including:

- Abraham Lincoln's wooden leg
- A group of really interesting acorns
- A cardboard box with a stain on the side that, when viewed in a certain light, looks amazingly like Robert Goulet
- The entire cast of *The Wizard of Oz*, preserved in formaldehyde
- Senator Joseph Biden's original hair
- A rock that the crew of the *Apollo 17* mission found on either the moon or a golf course near Phoenix, depending on which crew member you believe
- The Wright Brothers' original airplane, complete with Wilbur's original pee stain

. . . and much, much more. The best part of the Smithsonian collection is that you might be able to add to it! That's right: The Smithsonian is always looking for new items of Americana to put on exhibit, so when you visit, be sure to take along a box or two filled with stuff from around your house that you no longer need. The Smithsonian is very rich and will pay you **top dollar** for your Beanie Babies, Cabbage Patch dolls, Pokémon cards, refrigerator magnets, ceramic cats, Tupperware, T-shirts, empty beer bottles, etc. Just recently the Smithsonian paid an Akron, Ohio, man $7,500 for a set of **used tires** that he was about to throw away. You could probably pay for your entire trip to Washington just by cleaning out your garage!

When you're done touring the Smithsonian (allow fifteen to twenty minutes) head for the **National Gallery of Art,** which is a good place to go to the **bathroom.** Then it's on to the **Bureau of Engraving and Printing,** which prints all of the nation's **paper currency,** then packs it into bundles and trucks it to the garage of **Bill Gates.** A fun and very original thing to do here is to go up to a guard and ask if the Bureau is giving out any "free samples." Ha ha! This hilarious joke never fails to get a rise out of the guards and is well worth getting shot in the **leg** for.

Just down the street is the **Department of Infrastructure,** which was created during the Carter administration by a congressional act that, because it was passed during a hectic late-night session, most members of Congress actually believed was intended to declare **Yarn Safety Week.** The Department has since grown to seventeen thousand employees, and is tasked with the implementation of the facilitation of the amelioration of the prioritization of resource aggregation, allocation, and utilization. It has an excellent **cafeteria**.

Your tour of the Mall area ends with a stop at the **Department of Agriculture**, which is located in a building the size of **Connecticut**. This is an excellent place for you and your family to spend a day, wandering from office to office and asking employees what exactly the hell they **do**. Avoid the fifth and sixth floors, which since 1967 have been overrun by **aphids**.

As you continue west (or possibly east) on the Mall, you come to what is considered by many historians to be one of the pointiest things in all of Washington:

The Washington Monument

This monument to the "father of our country" is truly an example of what an artist can design in under five minutes if he is allowed to use only a pencil and a straight edge. Construction of the monument was begun in 1848 with the placement of the first stone, with the second stone being placed on top of that in 1850. At this point, work was halted for thirty years while the contractor was being treated by his chiropractor. The monument was finally completed in 1884, then transported to its current location by a team of really strong mules. Tragically, George Washington did not live long enough to see his completed monument, although at the dedication ceremony his son, Roger Washington, declared that it "looks exactly like him."

In 1998 the monument was closed for a massive

renovation project that involved the removal of more than six hundred thousand square yards of shag carpeting. The monument was reopened in 2000 with a ceremony capped by a spectacular display of skyrockets fired by British troops, who were subsequently recaptured and returned to their nursing home.

Today the monument is one of the capital's most popular tourist attractions, with seventeen million visitors per day ascending to the top on the original **elevator,** which is powered by static electricity and still uses the original **horsehair cable,** lovingly maintained by National Park Service personnel based permanently on the **ground.** To get to the top of the monument, simply go to the front of the long line of people waiting for the elevator and tell them that they can just step aside because you are an American **taxpayer** who is not going to spend another damn minute waiting in another damn **line,** dammit.

Assuming you make it down from the top of the monument alive, your next stop is the **Reflecting Pool,** a rectangular body of water that gets its name from the fact that, if you lean over and look into it, you can see—astonishing as it may sound—your own **face.** But don't spend too much time admiring yourself, because the Reflecting Pool is home to **Momba,** a legendary carp[11] who, after decades of eating high-calorie junk food thrown into the pool by tourists, has grown to nineteen hundred pounds, and who in March of 1997 suddenly lunged up and, in one gulp, swallowed an entire **pedestrian.** (Tragically, the victim was never identified, because he was the Secretary of the Interior.)

---

[11] "Legendary Carp" would be a good name for a rock band.

INCREDIBLE BUT TRUE!
WASHINGTON MONUMENT FACTS

An identical backup monument, constructed during the Cold War, is kept in a secret underground vault located in West Virginia.

The monument is actually only twenty-eight feet high, but appears much taller because of the earth's rotation.

The monument is home to one of the world's largest free-roaming colonies of head lice.

The official U.S. National Park Service nickname for the monument is "The Big Johnson."

The monument is precisely located such that, if you stand at the south side of the base at exactly noon on July 15, pretty soon you will be sweating like a mother.

Since construction was completed in 1884, the monument has fallen over only six times.

According to local legend, if you throw a cat from the top of the monument, it will soon strike the ground.

Lucille Ball (1911–1989) is buried under the monument.

(Source: Dan Rather)

Gazing somberly down at the Reflecting Pool
from a majestic vantage point directly to the west is
one of the most beloved and inspirational sights in
all of Washington: **Earl,** a guy who retired from the
plumbing-supply business in 1982 to devote himself
to his hobby, which is gazing somberly down at
things. Directly behind Earl, on most days, is the **Lincoln Memorial.**

A short distance away is the **Tidal Basin,** ringed by
cherry trees that every year produce **flowers,** an
event to which Washingtonians react as though it
were the **Second Coming of Christ.**

Historically, the Tidal Basin was the site of a really
wonderful true episode that occurred in 1974, featuring **Wilbur Mills,** a congressman from Arkansas[12]
who was chairman of the House Ways and Means
Committee and thus one of the most powerful politicians in the nation. The episode began when police
stopped a car that was being driven too fast, especially considering the fact that the time was 2 A.M.
and the car's lights were off. Inside the car, police
found Representative Mills, as well as a **woman**
who was definitely not **Mrs. Mills.** She turned out
to be **Annabel Battistella,** a stripper who per-
formed under the stage name **Fanne Foxe ("The Ar-
gentine Firecracker").** She got out of the car and,
for reasons that are still not clear, jumped into the
Tidal Basin.

As you can imagine, this caused quite a scandal.
But Representative Mills, unlike a certain other **sex-
crazed Arkansas politician** who shall remain **name-**

[12]Needless to say.

less, did not attempt to deny his relationship. In fact, his method of damage control was to travel to Boston with Miss Foxe and *appear on stage with her.* He later told the press that he did this "to dispel all these innuendoes."[13]

"I think I was right," he said. "Of course, I could be wrong."

Despite this courageous display of honesty, Representative Mills lost his committee chairmanship and left Congress pretty much in disgrace, which I think is a darned shame, considering that he is one of the few American politicians in modern history to actually accept responsibility for anything. In fact, I think there should be a **Wilbur Mills Monument** next to the Tidal Basin. I envision it as a statue of a portly man, with his hair mussed up and his tie askew. The statue would be delicately balanced on some kind of springs or hinges, so it would wobble in the wind, as though at any moment it was going to topple over into the water. At the bottom, carved in stone, this inscription would memorialize a phrase that is virtually never uttered in official Washington:

Of course, I could be wrong.

But getting back to reality: You'll continue your tour by heading over to one of the most imaginatively named buildings in the world:

[13] I am not making these quotes up.

The White House

The White House is located at 1600 Pennsylvania Avenue. Be sure you go to the right address, because the people at 1598 Pennsylvania Avenue, Melvin and Estelle Grundermuckle, have a really mean **dog.**

The White House was completed in 1829 and will be fully paid off in just 127 more mortgage payments. It is both the official residence and the office of the president of the United States, and as such it receives the Premium Movie cable-TV package. The **First Family's quarters** are on the second floor; the third floor is a **Kinko's.**

There are many fascinating sights to see in the White House, including the **Oval Office,** the **Lincoln Bedroom,** the **Chester A. Arthur Wastebasket,** the **Lyndon B. Johnson Executive Commode,** the **Richard M. Nixon Great Big Jar of Vaseline,** the **Monica Lewinsky Twin Carpet Indentations,** and the **Room They Always Show in Movies with the Big Conference Table Where the Generals Tell the President That Enemy Missiles Have Been Launched.** Unfortunately, you are not allowed to see any of these unless you have given the president's campaign a great big pile of **money.** As an ordinary dirtbag member of the public, all you see on the official tour are some rooms containing historic but ugly **furniture.** (Actually, these days, to see some of the nicer White House furniture, you will have to visit one of the **several residences** of Mr. and Mrs. Bill Clinton.)

The White House is open to the public every day except when it is being used to film the TV show

The West Wing. To take a tour, simply climb over the fence and hold very still until men come sprinting to assist you.

Once you're out of federal custody, it's time to conclude your tour by crossing the Potomac to Virginia and visiting:

The Pentagon

This amazing building, the headquarters of the American military, is a miracle of engineering: It was constructed for $50 million in 1943 by the Avocado Brothers Construction and Vending Machine Co., which built the entire structure in a single weekend and received payment in cash. It was supposed to be a normal building with four sides, but there was mustard on the plans.

Today the Pentagon remains the largest office building in the world, with 685 **drinking fountains,** which every day yield more than twelve thousand wads of **gum.** The Pentagon also boasts more than seventeen miles of **corridors;** there are people wandering around here still trying to deliver urgent memos pertaining to the **Normandy Invasion.**

The public may take a ninety-minute **walking tour** of the Pentagon, during which every visitor who promises that he or she is not a foreign spy is given a souvenir copy of the **nuclear missile launch codes.** At the end of the tour you will be asked to do some **push-ups** and then be aggressively pressured to join the **army.**

*   *   *

This concludes your tour of the nation's capital. I hope that it has helped you to realize that, as a citizen, *you* are the true "boss" of the federal government in every sense of the word, except the sense of having power or status or being allowed to enter most of the buildings. Nevertheless I'm sure that you'll leave the capital with a deeper appreciation of how your federal government works, so that the next time you pay your income tax, you'll have a big smile on your face. Of course, I could be wrong.

CHAPTER FIVE

The Presidential Election Process (or)

Goobers on Parade

THE UNITED STATES used to elect impressive presidents—guys like George Washington, Thomas Jefferson, Abraham Lincoln, and Thomas Edison. But it seems that, over the years, the quality of our presidential timber has declined; today we're pretty much satisfied if our president stays out of jail and occasionally emits a complete sentence.

In a way, this is good. It proves that we are not lying when we say, as we often do, that in the United States, *anybody* can be elected president, regardless of race, religion, or gender, as long as he is a middle-aged married white heterosexual male with no visible tattoos.

Also he has to be clearly a human being. This is why Steve Forbes, despite having the same net worth as Finland, could never get anybody other than his wife to vote for him. Steve had some good ideas, but when you watched him speak, with that weird smile and those unblinking eyes, you had trouble focusing on what he was saying, because you were worried that his face might suddenly peel away to reveal a circuit board.

But even though Steve didn't win the presidency, some pretty unimpressive guys *have* done it, which is why so many politicians sincerely believe that they have a legitimate shot. Their role model is Jimmy Carter. People tend to forget this, but before Jimmy became an admired house-building ex-president, he was, for a brief period back during the disco era, the actual president. Historians are still not sure how this happened. I mean, Jimmy is a good man, but he is also a man with the charisma of a cheese log. Yet he went from nowhere to becoming the *most powerful man in the world*. One day he's a semi-unknown politician cutting the ribbon to open the Moon Pie Festival; next thing you know, he's exchanging threats with the Soviet Union!

This story is very inspiring to a lot of guys stuck in dead-end, loser jobs such as governor or U.S. senator. They look at themselves in the mirror and they say: "Hey, why can't I be the president?"

And the mirror thinks: *Because you are a bozo.* Tragically, the mirror cannot talk.

And so every four years, many sincerely self-impressed presidential timbers call press conferences to declare that they are prepared to serve the nation. When they say "serve the nation," what they of course *mean* is that they want to be whisked around the nation in a motorcade, and fly on Air Force One, and be catered to by a large fawning entourage, and have an adoring public cheering and applauding and sometimes flashing its thong.

In other words, they want to be president for the same reason you do: It *would be cool*. When you're the president, you are *the man*. If your executive toilet gets clogged, you don't go looking for the plunger: You simply pick up the phone, push a button, say "My toilet is clogged," then hang up. Because you know that *action will be taken*. It will be taken even if you accidentally pushed the wrong button and were talking to the prime minister of Japan. Within hours, the White House will receive, out of the blue, a brand new solid-gold commode with a pearl-encrusted flush handle as a gift from the Japanese people. That's the kind of clout the president has!

The problem is that, to *become* the president, you have to *run* for president, which in the past few decades has become a brutally degrading experience involving unspeakable depths of pandering and sucking around for votes and money. It's a great big Suck-a-Thon, is what it is. No dignified person would voluntarily submit to it; the people who *do* submit to it are usually defective to begin with, and come out of the process moderately deranged, if not actively insane. One of these years we're going to elect a president whose first official act will be to launch nuclear strikes against Iowa and New Hampshire. And you wouldn't blame him, if you saw what presidential candidates go through, especially the ones who are considered "dark horses," which means they have essentially the same chance of being elected president as they do of winning the Preakness.

I've spent a lot of time out on the presidential campaign trail, doing what a professional journalist does, which is primarily sit around in bars listening

to other professional journalists present one another with irrefutable evidence that editors have the
intelligence of lunch meat. But sometimes I go out
and watch the actual process of presidential politics.
And let me tell you, it is not what you see on TV.

What you see on TV, usually, is a candidate standing in front of a group of voters who are listening
with interest as the candidate lays out his program
for health care, child care, pig care, lawn care, or
whatever kind of care the candidate thinks these
particular voters care about sufficiently to want from
the government. That image is dreary enough, but
it's nowhere near as bad as the reality of presidential
campaigning, which largely consists of the candidate schlepping around from pathetic event to pathetic event, desperately trying to locate voters who
are willing to pay any kind of attention to him at all.

I'm thinking now of a cold, gray New Hampshire
January afternoon in 1984, when I followed a presidential timber named Reubin Askew as he went on a
lonely, desperate quest around a New Hampshire
shopping mall, looking for somebody, *anybody*, to
shake hands with. For those of you who are not into
Trivial Political Pursuit, Reubin Askew was once the
governor of Florida, and was once considered to be
an intelligent, competent, and sane human being.
But then he got it into his head that he could be
president. (Why not? Jimmy Carter did!)

So off Reubin went to New Hampshire, hoping to
catch fire with the electorate. When I found him, he
was wandering aimlessly around the shopping mall
while several of his campaign workers went around
trying to hunt down voters for him to ignite. They'd

go up to some harried woman shopper with three small children and five large shopping bags, and they'd say, "Would you like to meet Reubin Askew? He's running for president!" They'd gesture toward Reubin, who was lurking a few yards away, trying to look presidential—as though at any moment the president of Egypt was going to show up and have high-level talks with Reubin in the Chick-fil-A. After an agonizingly awkward pause, the shopper—who, like most New Hampshire residents, considered presidential hopefuls to be about as exciting as road salt—would shake her head and trudge away, leaving the Askew juggernaut to try to ignite some-body else.

It happened that 1984 was a banner year for Democratic presidential candidates who were un-likely to garner any votes outside of their immediate families. Among the other dark horses clomping around New Hampshire in search of voters to inflict their visions on were:

• Senator Ernest "Fritz" Hollings of either North or South Carolina, whose distinguishing characteris-tic was that he sounded *exactly* like Foghorn T. Leghorn, the Warner Brothers cartoon rooster.[1] In candidate debates, when Fritz was explaining

[1]True fact: At a 1984 campaign appearance in Portsmouth, New Hampshire, some Hollings campaign workers sang the following song, to the tune of "Do Wah Diddy Diddy (Dum Diddy Do)" by Manfred Mann:
He looks good! (Looks good!)
He stands tall! (Stands tall!)
Looks good, stands tall
And he has a Southern drawl!

how he would balance the federal budget, you found yourself unable to pay attention, because you were expecting that at any moment he'd be attacked by an angry Warner Brothers cartoon dog, which at the last instant would reach the end of his chain and be yanked violently backward, at which point Fritz would hit him with a big cartoon baseball bat.

- The Reverend Jesse Jackson, who had acquired a reputation for great eloquence because he could really rouse a crowd, but whose speeches, when you analyzed what they actually *said*, often did not make a ton of sense. You'd go to hear him speak, and you'd think, "Wow!" And then later you'd review your notes, and you'd realize that his most mesmerizing lines appeared to have been produced by the Random Rhyming Big Word Generator ("The *revolution* of the *institution* depends on the *evolution* of the *Constitution!*").

- Senator Alan Cranston of California, who looked more like a corpse than many actual cemetery residents, and who had apparently decided to give himself a more youthful look by dyeing his little fringe of remaining hair with Rust-Oleum.

- Senator John Glenn of Ohio, who was a true space hero, but who had all the oratorical skills of a pump motor, so that his speeches were punctuated by the thud of audience members being rendered unconscious and toppling face-first to the floor.

- George McGovern, who had already proven, as the 1972 Democratic nominee, that he could attract voters from all across the political spectrum, provided that they lived in Boston or its immediate suburbs.

• A person named "Vance Hartke."

The hot new Democratic name in 1984 was Senator Gary Hart of Colorado, who suddenly, out of nowhere, became hugely popular for no evident reason, like Britney Spears. This is the reality of presidential politics: Somebody gets hot, and it usually has nothing to do with his positions on the issues, assuming he has some. It's some kind of inexplicable chemical thing between the candidate and the voters, and in 1984 it happened with Hart. Everywhere he went, he drew large, excited, squealing crowds. You'd ask people, "Why do you support Hart?" And they'd say, "I like his ideas!" Then you'd ask, "Which ideas of his do you like?" And they'd say, "You know! His . . . ideas!"

I was never clear myself on what Hart's ideas were, although I do remember he talked a lot about plutonium. Basically, I think people liked him because they thought he looked and sounded kind of cool.

I believe that how a candidate looks and sounds is way more important to the voters than his position on anything, which is why the public periodically decides that it likes some politician who totally disagrees with some other politician that the public also likes. The public to this day is crazy mad for John F. Kennedy, not because of his policies—nobody has a clue what his policies were—but because . . . he had class! He was handsome! His wife was beautiful! He was President Beatle!

The public also liked Ronald Reagan, not because

the public was suddenly conservative, but because
Reagan looked and sounded like a nice guy—maybe
not the sharpest dart in the board, but a regular and
decent fellow, who made you feel like your nice old
Uncle Bob had somehow wound up running the
country. And the public liked Bill Clinton, at least at
first, not because the public was suddenly liberal,
but because the public found Clinton to be outgoing
and friendly, and so the public forgave him for also
being a complete horn dog who, given half a chance,
would shag the public's wife.

But getting back to 1984: Hart was clearly the
most attractive candidate, the only one with even a
remote chance of beating Ronald Reagan, so naturally the Democrats selected: Walter Mondale. When
Mondale accepted the nomination, he wooed the
voters by informing them—in that intensely nasal,
concrete-penetrating voice of his, which seemed to
emanate from huge sinus cavities made of stainless
steel—that if they elected him as president, his first
move would be to jack up their income taxes.

Walter, you sweet-talker!

This was back when the Democrats' strategy was to
pick candidates who were definitely going to lose.[2] In
1988, after front-runner Gary Hart, Man of Ideas, decided that it would be a good presidential idea to
have his photograph taken in Bimini with a hot babe

[2]Later on the Republicans adopted the sure-loser strategy, most
notably in 1996, when, to combat Bill Clinton, the smoothest, hug-
gingest, slickest-talking president in decades, they nominated Bob
Dole, who, no matter what he was actually saying, always managed
to sound like a cranky old geezer who suspected his audience of
having stolen his newspaper.

in his lap, the Democrats settled on . . . Michael Dukakis! Mr. Excitement! Dukakis was an intelligent man, but he was also a man who had essentially the same range of facial expressions as an iguana. He did not fire up an audience. When he was speaking, the audience expected that at any moment his tongue would come flicking out and snag a passing insect. Dukakis also had the incredibly bad judgment to be videotaped riding in an army tank with his head poking up out of the hatch, wearing a helmet that made him look like Captain Dork of the Weenie Patrol. If this tank had ever gone into battle, it would have rolled right over the enemy, which would have been lying helplessly on the ground, wetting its pants.

But the real quality entertainment of the 1988 campaign came from the Republican side, which featured, among other contenders, The Extremely Reverend Pat "Pat" Robertson. One of my all-time favorite campaign moments was watching the Reverend Robertson make a stop in Leon, Iowa, when he was traveling across the state by bus. He was supposed to be traveling by helicopter, but a snowstorm had forced him to change his plans.

Perhaps you're wondering why the Reverend Robertson didn't just make the storm go away, the way he claimed to have done in 1985, when Hurricane Gloria was headed toward his Virginia headquarters, and he prayed about it, and at the last minute the hurricane veered away. This was a great miracle, only slightly tarnished by the fact that Gloria went on to smash into the Northeast and cause several deaths. (Not that I'm blaming the

Reverend Robertson: At that point, he was no longer steering.)

But in 1988 the Reverend Robertson was not taking an active role in the weather, because he wanted to project the image of a thoughtful and capable leader, rather than the image of a raving loon. When I saw him, his bus had stopped for a campaign appearance at the largest factory in Leon, which manufactured, of all products, ladies' lingerie. So there was the Reverend Robertson, Mr. Family Values, standing uncomfortably in the middle of a vast forest of semitransparent underwear. A small group of lingerie workers timidly emerged, deerlike, from this forest to watch quietly as the Reverend Robertson declared that he was in favor of the family, thereby setting himself sharply apart from all the candidates who were against the family. Then the Reverend Robertson went back to his bus, and the factory workers melted back into the lingerie, and life returned to normal in Leon for another four years.

As entertaining as the Reverend Extremely was, though, the ticket that the Republicans finally picked in 1988 was, as a team, one of the most comical duos we have ever had running the nation. At the top, regularly emitting statements that had the entire nation going *Huh?*, you had George Herbert Walker Vanderbilt Pierce-Worcestershire Kennebunkport Bush. There has always been something wonderfully *goofy* about this man. We have all heard, endlessly, about the language problems of his son, our current president, George W. Bush. Experts have speculated on why W has so much trouble forming a sentence that involves both nouns *and* verbs. To me the answer is obvious: *He grew up listening to his father talk.* Think back to some of the statements that the elder Bush made while he was the actual president of the United States:

On a song by the Nitty Gritty Dirt Band: "I said to them there's another one that the Nitty Ditty Nitty Gritty Great Bird and it says if you want to see a rainbow you've got to stand a little rain."

On the First Lady: "Everybody is talking about Barbara, we miss her very, very much. And I told her I didn't need her, I was not going to throw up."

On his health: "So don't feel sorry for, don't cry for me, Argentina."

On his message: "But the message: I care."

On extending unemployment benefits: "If a frog had wings, he wouldn't hit his tail on the ground. Too hypothetical."

In 1988, when, as vice president, Bush was campaigning for the Republican presidential nomination, I observed him at a construction site near Miami, where his motorcade had stopped for what his press secretary had said would be an "impromptu" stop, which was as impromptu as the Hoover Dam. It was the usual campaign scene: Bush shook hands with construction workers while the Secret Service stood around looking alert, in case assassins suddenly came lunging out of the Portolets. Then the vice president saw a potential photo opportunity in the form of a large piece of construction equipment called a "vibratory roller," which is basically a great big studly masculine steamroller on steroids.

Realizing that this was a good chance to look presidential, Bush climbed up on the vibratory roller next to the operator and, to the obvious horror of the Secret Service, began yanking on levers in an impromptu manner, thereby causing the vibratory roller to violently whomp the ground, raising a cloud of dust and forcing TV camerapersons to scurry for cover. When the nervous-looking operator finally got the machine stopped, Vice President Bush climbed down, put his arm around the operator, and said—I swear— "He taught me everything I know about vibrators."

But when it came to eloquence, George Bush was Winston Churchill compared with his vice president, the legendary J. Danforth Quayle. You never knew what Dan was going to say next, and the wonderful thing was, *Dan clearly didn't know either.* He'd be asked a question, and he'd start talking, and you could see in his eyes that he was thinking, *Ohmigod I'm talking and I HAVE NO EARTHLY IDEA WHAT I'M TRYING TO SAY! I DON'T EVEN KNOW WHAT I'M SAYING RIGHT NOW!* There is no other explanation for some of Vice President Quayle's legendary observations, such as:

On the possibility of life on Mars: "We have seen pictures where there are canals, we believe, and water. If there is water, that means there is oxygen. If oxygen, that means we can breathe."[3]

[3]When Quayle made this statement, he was *Chairman of the National Space Council.*

On the mind: "What a waste it is to lose one's mind, or not to have a mind as being very wasteful. How true that is."

On success: "If we don't succeed, we run the risk of failure."

On the vice presidency: "One word sums up probably the responsibility of any vice president, and that one word is 'to be prepared.' "

Yes, the Bush-Quayle administration was a bonanza for us humor writers. But for sheer hilarity of White House hijinks, we may never top the glorious eight years of the administration of President Bill "Mr. Legacy" Clinton. I mean, with this guy in charge, wacky stuff was *always* happening. And whenever it did, Washington would transform itself into yet another episode of a long-running situation comedy, with lovable, familiar characters and a predictable, three-act plot:

Act One: There would be some scandalous development, such as rumors that a pizza-delivering intern had been sampling the presidential pepperoni; or the discovery that missing files, wanted in a criminal investigation, had suddenly turned up in the residential part of the White House and *nobody had a clue how they got there*, as though the White House residence were the kind of low-security, public place, like a bus station, where random strangers were always wandering in and leaving things.

Act Two: After the scandalous development became public, the president would get all somber and semi-weepy, and bite his lip, and declare that the whole thing was caused by a miscommunication or a misunderstanding or a misinterpretation or a Miss Lewinsky, but technically, *legally*, no laws had been broken, and that if the Republicans wanted to engage in a Partisan Witch-Hunt as part of a Massive Right Wing Conspiracy, then they could go right ahead, but he, the *president*, was going to keep on doing the job that the American people elected him to do, namely travel around the country raising money for the Democratic party and give everybody within reach a great big old hug.

Act Three: The Republicans, seeing a chance to finally get rid of a president whom they detested more than anything in the world except rap music, and realizing that they had the law *and* the evidence clearly on their side, would put on their thinking caps and come up with a political strategy that was absolutely guaranteed to backfire and make them look even more pompous, hypocritical, and clueless than before. The Republicans were like the cartoon character Wile E. Coyote; at the end of the show, the anvil *always* landed smack on their own heads, while President Semen Stain streaked off into the sunset with a carefree *meep meep*.

We had eight wonderfully entertaining years of this, climaxing with a spectacular finale. You had Bill staying up all night issuing pardons to everybody except Charles Manson. And then you had the Clintons, when they finally left, taking with them, all kinds of parting gifts, as White House curators discovered the next day ("Hey! Where the heck is the Lincoln Bedroom?").

As a humor columnist, I miss Bill Clinton. I started to miss him before he even left office, during the grim death march of the 2000 presidential campaign, wherein it gradually dawned upon the nation that their next president was going to be either:

- Al Gore, whose entire political philosophy seemed to be that everything his opponent proposed was a risky scheme, and who had developed this incredibly annoying, condescending manner of speech that made him sound, when he spoke to us, as though he were addressing a herd of unusually stupid sheep. ("This is a risky scheme! It is bad! Baaad! B*aaaaaaaa*...")
- George W. Bush, whose entire political philosophy seemed to be whatever he had just read on a three-by-five card written by an adviser, and who often sounded as though he had the *brain* of a sheep. (Actual quote: "There is madmen in the world, and there are terror.")

Those were our choices in the 2000 election: We could elect President Annoying or we could elect President Dope.

Here's the thing: I have actually spent time in social settings with both Al Gore and George W. Bush. I'm not saying I got to know them well, but I will say that Gore seemed more natural in person and Bush seemed smarter. They were nothing like the two over-programmed androids I saw debating each other on TV, both of them desperately trying to get all their memorized sound bites in. This is why our political campaigns have become so awful: Most candidates believe that the only way to win is to *never* say anything spontaneous or funny or thought-provoking or edgy, but instead to endlessly regurgitate some market-tested, focus-grouped, fundamentally meaningless wad of rhetorical sludge ("Building a Bridge to the Twentieth Century!" "A Reformer with Results!" "Tastes Great!" "Less Filling!").

If a normal person engaged in this kind of behavior—robotically repeating some simplistic statement no matter what he was asked—he would be viewed as mentally ill. But when candidates do it, they are viewed as being "on message," which is considered good professional politics. Because it works! The voters buy it! At least the ones who actually vote do. But there are fewer and fewer of those, aren't there?

You hear a lot of whining from editorial writers about declining voter participation in presidential elections. The gist of this whining is that there's something wrong with the voters. But look at the *candidates*. Maybe the voters aren't voting because they recognize that our current political system, which has been created by and for paid political professionals, is almost guaranteed to present us with a choice between two suit-wearing Muppets.

What can we do to bring the voters back? I have some suggestions. The most important is:

1. Inject Honesty into Political Campaigns

I am not using the word "inject" figuratively, here. I am talking about the mandatory injection of large dosages of sodium pentothal—also known as "truth serum"—into the veins of all presidential candidates. Under my plan, every candidate would be accompanied at all times by a syringe-toting physician employed by the Federal Elections Commission, who would be responsible for making sure that the candidate had enough sodium pentothal in his bloodstream to ensure that he told voters what he was actually thinking.

This would greatly improve the campaign process. To understand how, let's consider a specific example; namely, the way candidates in the Iowa caucuses deal with the ethanol issue.

Ethanol is some kind of chemical that has something to do with using corn as automobile fuel. The Iowans, who have corn out the wazoo, are obsessed with it, and will insist on growing it in huge quantities even when nobody wants it.

So when a presidential hopeful is campaigning in Iowa, at virtually every stop there will come a ritual moment when some farmer wearing a baseball-style cap with the brand name of a pesticide on the front will demand to know where the candidate stands on ethanol. It is considered mandatory for the candidate to respond by making the following ritual points:

- Farmers are the backbone of this great nation.
- This nation has become too dependent on oil from the Middle East.
- The Middle East is a foreign place containing foreigners.
- Those are not Americans, over there in the Middle East!

- Whereas American farmers *are* Americans, and let's not forget it.
- Therefore, as president, the candidate will make it his highest priority to get more Americans to fuel their automobiles with corn from Iowa, which is an American state located in America, the very country of which farmers are the backbone.
- Also the candidate would spend billions of federal dollars on programs to develop and promote new corn-based products, such as corn-flavored ice cream, corn-based roofing shingles, corn-powered computers, etc.
- Also he would spend hours each day worshiping at a Sacred Corn Shrine installed in the Oval Office.

And so on. All the candidates—regardless of where they are on the political spectrum—kiss major farmer butt on the corn/ethanol issue while in Iowa. And of course the instant the caucuses are over, they all relegate corn to its rightful place on their list of priorities, which is: Nowhere. Then they move on to New Hampshire to pretend they care about some issue that New Hampshire voters care about, such as federal slush insurance.

Imagine how much more *meaningful* this whole process would be if the candidates were all juiced to the gills on sodium pentothal. Imagine if, when the corn farmer asked the ritual ethanol question, the candidates responded by *saying what they actually felt*. It would probably be something along these lines:

FARMER: I'm a corn farmer, and I just want to know where you stand on ethanol.

CANDIDATE: Hey, Gomer, I'll tell you what you can do with your corn.

At first, the Iowans would be shocked. They would vow to support other candidates. But if *all* the candidates were being honest, it would eventually dawn on the corn farmers that, despite all the lies they've heard from pandering presidential hopefuls in the past, *nobody* who is not a corn farmer cares about the ethanol "issue." Eventually they would say to themselves, "Gosh, I guess the president of the United States has more important things to think about!" And the nation would be a better place.

I don't mean to single out Iowans. I believe the entire American electorate, which is infested with whining special interest groups expecting to have their behinds smooched, would benefit tremendously from hearing plain-spoken, frank views expressed by heavily drugged candidates.

I'm picturing a scene, here:

The candidate is at one of those phony "town meeting" campaign events, and the mandatory earnest young person asks the candidate what he would do to improve the educational system. The candidate answers that as far as he can tell, the biggest problem with our educational system is that it is trying to educate young people who are, to judge from the music they listen to, stupid. Warming to the topic, the candidate says that if our young people don't have the brain power to get good scores on their SATs, maybe we should ship them abroad in exchange for some foreign students who can get the job done.

Then the mandatory police chief gets up and asks what the candidate would do about crime. And the candidate answers that he favors the death penalty for anybody found guilty of graduating from law school.

Then the mandatory old person gets up and asks what the candidate is going to do for senior citizens. And the candidate answers that he is going to take away their Social Security if they don't learn to drive a little faster and switch off their damn turn signals.

Then the mandatory pro- and anti-abortion rights people get up to make preachy statements, and the candidate says: "Why don't you people just go outside and whack one another with your signs and leave the rest of us ALONE?"

Then the mandatory concerned mother gets up and asks how the candidate feels about drugs. And the candidate answers, thanks, but he doesn't need any right now; he's doing fine with the sodium pentothal.

Wouldn't that be *great*? Wouldn't you, as a voter, pay a lot more attention to a candidate who was not capable of lying to you? Just imagine how much fun it would be to watch a debate involving *several* presidential candidates who could not avoid telling the truth (newspaper headline: CANDIDATES, IN DEBATE, AGREE THEY ALL BASICALLY JUST WANT ATTENTION).

But chemically induced honesty is only the first prong of my multipronged program for improving presidential campaigns. The second is:

2. Require Candidates to Wear Donor Logos

Have you ever watched auto races on television? Have you noticed that the drivers wear uniforms plastered with the logos of the companies that sponsor them? Has it ever occurred to you that we could do something similar with presidential candidates? That's right: *We could crash them into walls at two hundred miles per hour.*

No, as much fun as that would be, what I'm actually proposing is that we require candidates to wear signs clearly identifying who is paying them to hold their current set of opinions. This would clear up a lot of confusion. For example, Al Gore often passionately declared his commitment to public schools, which was puzzling, because he sent his own personal children to exclusive private junior and senior high schools. Think how much clearer the situation would have been if Al had been wearing a teachers union logo the size of a dinner plate. And imagine how much easier it would be to understand George W. Bush's environmental policies if he had an oil company sign tattooed on his forehead. You wouldn't even have to listen to what the candidates said! You could just read their logos!

And speaking of getting the candidates' messages across, the next prong of my program for campaign reform is:

3. Make the Presidential Debates More Interesting

In recent years, the total national viewership of televised presidential debates has consisted of Cokie Roberts.[4] Normal American citizens would rather watch a bug crawling across the darkened TV screen than a couple of stiffs in dark suits standing behind lecterns blurting memorized points and promising to lead America.

One sure way to improve viewership for debates would be to allow the public to call a toll-free number and vote for a winner, then immediately, on camera, electrocute the loser. Unfortunately, this would probably violate some legal technicality. But I see no reason why we couldn't expand the scope of the debate to include swimsuit and talent competitions. Or how about a strip quiz on world events, wherein every time a candidate gets an answer wrong, he has to remove an article of clothing? How about giving each candidate a slip of paper with a mystery phrase, such as "monkey nostrils," that he must work into every answer he gives? How about having Billy Crystal do an opening monologue? How about making the candidates crouch behind the lecterns and conduct the entire debate with sock puppets? How about having each candidate get into a tub of Jell-O and wrestle Yasir Arafat?

These are just some suggestions off the top of my head. I'm sure you can think of some equally good ones, once you've had as many beers as I have. Which brings us to our next campaign-reform prong:

[4]Whose name can be rearranged to spell "I broke corset."

4. Require That All Campaign Advertisements Be Performed Exclusively by the Swamp Critters in the Budweiser Commercials

In other words, the candidates could run the same ads they do now—the candidate standing with his or her family, the candidate looking with concern at a group of senior citizens, etc.—except that every character, including the candidate, would be played by a frog, a lizard, or a ferret. The ferret would do all the voice-overs, because he is incomprehensible. Speaking of which, the final prong in our campaign-reform fork is:

5. Somewhere in Every Chapter, There Has to Be Some Giant Prehistoric Zucchini

CHAPTER SIX

A Modern American Political Campaign (or)

Seven Weeks of Truth in Advertising

Week One

TV ANNOUNCER: Congressman Bob Humpty. For fourteen years, he's been fighting for us in Washington.

(Bob Humpty, in rolled-up shirtsleeves, talking to a group of people, with the U.S. Capitol in the background. Humpty is making forceful, decisive hand gestures. The people are listening with great interest. There is no sound, so we cannot tell that the people are Norwegian tourists and he is giving them directions to the subway.)

ANNOUNCER: Bob Humpty. A husband. A father. A man with hair.

(Humpty with family, dog, hair. Everybody is smiling. The dog is radiant.)

ANNOUNCER: Let's keep Bob Humpty fighting for us. I
don't mean for me *personally*, of course. I'm a professional announcer who lives in New York and
has not voted since 1978.

(Close-up of Bob Humpty.)

BOB HUMPTY: I'm Bob Humpty. I want to keep fighting
for you in Washington, where I own a nice house.

(In large letters, the words "BOB HUMPTY. FIGHTING
FOR YOU.")

ANNOUNCER: Bob Humpty. (Significant pause.) He's
Bob Humpty.

Week Two

ANNOUNCER: Bob Humpty *says* he wants to fight for
you.

(Grainy black-and-white photo of Bob Humpty, looking
like a vampire with heartburn.)

ANNOUNCER: But as you can tell by how sneaky he
looks in this photograph, and by the skepticism in
my professional announcer voice, Bob Humpty is
not telling the truth. The facts are that in 1997,
Bob Humpty voted to allow special interests in the
nursing-home industry to increase their profits by
feeding senior citizens a diet consisting exclu-
sively of hamster-cage waste.

(Gaunt, elderly woman looking down sadly at a plate of dirty wood shavings.)

ANNOUNCER: Bill Dumpty thinks it's time for a change.

(Soft-focus close-up of Bill Dumpty, looking sincere.)

BILL DUMPTY: I'm Bill Dumpty, and I think it's wrong to let senior citizens starve.

(Bill Dumpty with an elderly woman. He hands her a Whopper Junior. She takes it gratefully.)

ANNOUNCER: Bill Dumpty. Let's send a caring fighter to Washington.

(In large letters, the words "BILL DUMPTY. A CARING FIGHTER.")

ANNOUNCER: Bill Dumpty. *(Significant pause.)* Otherwise, your mother will die.

Week Three

ANNOUNCER: Bob Humpty talks about the issues.

(Close-up of Bob Humpty, looking sad.)

BOB HUMPTY: It's a shame that Bill Dumpty has resorted to negative campaign ads filled with lies and distortions and subliminal messages urging children to have sex. I've always run positive campaigns focused on the issues, and you have my word that I always will. Although I have no control over what the professional announcer says.

ANNOUNCER: Bill Dumpty *says* he'll fight for you.

(Hideous grainy black-and-white photo of Bill Dumpty in which he appears to have at least three eyes.)

ANNOUNCER: But the truth is that Bill Dumpty has been taking money from special interests, which are bad.

(A rapid montage of what appear to be newspaper clippings. The stories are illegible, but among the visible headlines are DUMPTY TAKES MONEY FROM SPECIAL INTERESTS, DUMPTY A BIG FAT LIAR, and DUMPTY HELD IN CHURCH ARSON.)

ANNOUNCER: And Bill Dumpty's negative ads are lying about Bob Humpty's voting record. The truth is that Bob Humpty spent all of 1997 in a coma.

(Photo montage: Newspaper headlines stating HUMPTY IN COMA, HUMPTY TO SPEND ALL OF 1997 IN COMA, HUMPTY OBVIOUSLY CAN'T VOTE BECAUSE HE IS IN COMA, etc., followed by photo of Bob Humpty lying in a hospital bed, his eyes closed, as his dog licks him sadly.)

ANNOUNCER: And even then, Bob Humpty fought for senior citizens.

(An elderly woman standing next to Bob Humpty's co-matose body, gratefully shaking his limp hand.)

BOB HUMPTY: I don't want to use the kind of negative campaign tactics practiced by my opponent and his special interest friends with ties to organized crime. I want to keep talking about the issues, and fighting for you against the special interests in Washington.

(Bob Humpty, with the U.S. Capitol in the background, punching a fat man wearing a name tag that says SPECIAL INTEREST.)

ANNOUNCER: Bob Humpty. *(Significant pause.)* Because that's what it says in this script.

Week Four

ANNOUNCER: Bob Humpty says he wants to run a positive campaign. I know this because I do the professional announcing for both candidates in this race. But the truth is that Bob Humpty is running the most negative campaign in history, according to these actual newspaper headlines.

(Montage of headlines: HUMPTY RUNNING MOST NEGATIVE CAMPAIGN IN HISTORY, HUMPTY A BAD MAN, THESE ARE ACTUAL NEWSPAPER HEADLINES, etc.)

ANNOUNCER: Bill Dumpty thinks we've had enough.

(Bill Dumpty, wearing casual clothes in earth tones, standing in a sunlit meadow, stroking a worshipful dog. It appears to be the same dog used in the Bob Humpty ads.)

BILL DUMPTY: I'm Bill Dumpty, and I think we've had enough of Bob Humpty's negative campaign distortions, paid for by special interests bent on destroying the planet.

(Grainy black-and-white photograph of Bob Humpty shaking hands with Darth Vader.)

BILL DUMPTY: I don't think that's the kind of leadership we need. I think we need the kind of leadership who wears casual earth-tone clothes and is stroking this dog, which tested well with focus groups. I love animals, which unfortunately is more than I can say for my opponent.

(Grainy black-and-white photo of Bob Humpty hitting a kitten with a hammer.)

ANNOUNCER: Let's send the message to Bob Humpty that we're sick and tired of the negative campaigning and the brutal attacks on furred baby animals. Let's send a positive, caring, earth-tone wearer to fight the special interests in Washington. Let's elect Bob Humpty.

SECOND ANNOUNCER (whispering): No! Bill Dumpty!

ANNOUNCER: That's what I meant.

Week Five

ANNOUNCER: Bill Dumpty has been distorting Bob Humpty's record with his negative campaign ads paid for by special interest extremist groups.

(*Grainy black-and-white photograph of Bill Dumpty laughing gaily, with his arm around Adolf Hitler.*)

ANNOUNCER: But the saddest thing about Bill Dumpty's negative campaign has been his allegations about animal cruelty. It's lucky for him that Bob Humpty is running such a positive campaign, or we would tell you some pretty shocking things about Bill Dumpty and animal cruelty.

(*Grainy but explicit black-and-white photograph of Bill Dumpty sexually assaulting a sheep.*)

ANNOUNCER: Bob Humpty thinks we've had enough of Bill Dumpty's negative ads and distortions.

(*Close-up of Bob Humpty, looking very sincere.*)

BOB HUMPTY: I'm Bob Humpty, and I think it's time to stop name-calling and start talking about where we stand on the issues. I believe it's wrong to have sex with *any* kind of farm animal. I realize that my opponent disagrees with me. But I think we can debate this issue in a positive manner, without negativity and lies and threats by my opponent to kidnap my baby daughter.

(Bob Humpty protectively holding frightened-looking infant.)

ANNOUNCER: Bob Humpty. (Significant pause.) Right?

Week Six

ANNOUNCER: Bob Humpty *says* he wants to talk about the issues.

(Close-up photograph of the head of a praying mantis, labeled BOB HUMPTY.)

ANNOUNCER: Then why is Bob Humpty telling lies about Bill Dumpty? Bill Dumpty is a good man.

(Bill Dumpty shaking hands with a smiling Jesus Christ.)

ANNOUNCER: The facts are that since Bob Humpty went to Washington, more than 350 million people around the world have died from various causes, including disease, famine, earthquakes, and machete attacks.

(The words OVER 350 MILLION DEAD superimposed on top of a grainy black-and-white photograph of Bob Humpty.)

ANNOUNCER: Coincidence? Not according to these realistic-looking headlines.

(Newspaper headlines saying HUMPTY LINKED TO 350 MILLION DEATHS and NOT A COINCIDENCE.)

ANNOUNCER: Bill Dumpty thinks there's a better way.

(Close-up of Bill Dumpty. He has a halo.)

BILL DUMPTY: Unlike my opponent, I think it's wrong for people to die.

(Bill Dumpty touches a dead senior citizen, who sits up in the casket, smiles, and shakes Bill Dumpty's hand.)

ANNOUNCER: Bill Dumpty. *(Significant pause.)* I'm quitting this announcer job. I'm going to do something more honest, like rob graves.

Week Seven

Congressional Race Ends in Draw; Voters Choose Neither Candidate

MUNG CITY (AP)—In what officials here called an unprecedented outcome, neither candidate for Congress from the 763rd congressional district received a single vote in Tuesday's election.

The complete lack of turnout was especially surprising in view of the massive TV advertising campaigns run by both the incumbent, U.S. Rep. Bob Humpty (R-D), and his challenger, Bill Dumpty (D-R). Apparently, even the candidates themselves failed to cast ballots.

"This is the worst case of voter apathy I've ever seen," said Election Commissioner C. Wardell Crumpet. "It makes you wonder what's wrong with people in this country."

CHAPTER SEVEN

The Making of the President 2000 (or)

Let's Give Florida Back to Spain (Assuming Spain Will Take It)

YEARS FROM NOW, when history students look back on the presidential election of 2000, they will remark: "Boy, was *that* ever historic!"

They will be using the word "historic" in the sense of "stupid." They will find it hard to believe that the official procedure for filling the world's most important job involved, at one point, low-level Florida politicians sitting around squinting at pieces of cardboard, trying to figure out what on earth the voters were thinking when they did whatever they did in the voting booth.

DEMOCRATIC OFFICIAL (*holding up a ballot*): This one looks to me like it has a dimple. See? Next to Gore's name?

REPUBLICAN OFFICIAL (*squinting*): I wouldn't call that a dimple. It's more of, like, a spot.

DEMOCRATIC OFFICIAL: OK, but it could very well be

an *intentional* spot, and it's definitely next to Gore. I think it's a Gore spot.

REPUBLICAN OFFICIAL: I don't know that I would go so far as . . . wait! It's moving!

DEMOCRATIC OFFICIAL *(looking closer)*: My God, it is! It's . . . it's some kind of bug!

REPUBLICAN OFFICIAL: It's crawling toward Bush! It's a Bush bug!

DEMOCRATIC OFFICIAL: Wait a minute! Now it's crawling toward . . . Buchanan!

(The two officials exchange meaningful looks. After glancing around to see if anybody is watching, the Democrat brushes the bug off the ballot, onto the floor. The Republican stomps on it.)

DEMOCRATIC OFFICIAL: So that's one vote for Gore . . .

REPUBLICAN OFFICIAL: And one for Bush.

(They nod, then pick up the next ballot.)

DEMOCRATIC OFFICIAL: Now on this one, when I hold it at a certain angle, I'm definitely seeing a shadow. See it? Next to Gore?

REPUBLICAN OFFICIAL: You're making that shadow with your finger.

DEMOCRATIC OFFICIAL: Yes, but it's an *intentional* shadow.

And so on. The ballot mind-reading was just part of the bizarreness of the 2000 election. While these people were trying to discern the deep electoral significance of semipregnant chads, dandruff flecks, blobs of denture adhesive, semen stains,[1] etc., the streets outside were filled with irate protesters, winning converts to their viewpoints via the always effective tactic of shouting mindless slogans until their shirt fronts were drenched with spittle.

Needless to say, these protesters included the Reverend Jesse "Love Child" Jackson and the Reverend Al Sharpton, both of whom become filled with righteous anger pretty much whenever anything happens anywhere. If a meteorite swarm crashed into downtown Cleveland, Jesse and Al would be there within hours, proclaiming that (*a*) a disproportionate number of the meteorites landed on minorities, and (*b*) this was *clearly deliberate.*

But what was weird in the Florida election quagmire was that a bunch of the protesters were *Republicans.* Yes! The downtrodden oppressed GOP masses! They were out there marching in their active leisurewear, carrying signs and yelling traditional Republican protest chants such as:

> Give us what we want, y'all
> Or else we'll make the Dow Jones fall!

And:

> What do we want?
> JUSTICE!
> When do we want it?
> BEFORE OUR 3:45 P.M. TEE TIME!

---

[1] I would not rule this out.

Oh, it was a zoo, all right, and it quickly turned the United States political system into an international laughingstock. We were being mocked not only by traditional American-bashing nations such as France, but also by primitive third-world nations that elect their leaders by determining which of the candidates can lift the heaviest pig.[2]

The question is: How did we get into this mess? And what should we do about it?

One thing we obviously need to do—I have been advocating this for years—is fire a couple of medium-size missiles at France. But that will only make us feel better. It will not eliminate the underlying causes of the 2000 election mess. To do that, we need to take some serious, practical steps. Step one is:

1. Kick Florida, or at Least South Florida, Out of the Union

I don't say this lightly. I personally live in South Florida, and if we got kicked out of the union, I would no longer enjoy the many benefits of United States citizenship, such as . . .

OK, here's one: When I purchase a food item at the supermarket, I can be confident that the label will state how much riboflavin is in it. The United States government requires this, and for a good reason, which is: I have no idea. I don't even know what riboflavin is. I do know I eat a lot of it. For example, I

[2]Actually, this makes as much sense as the Electoral College.

often start the day with a hearty Kellogg's strawberry Pop-Tart, which has, according to the label, a ribo-flavin rating of 10 percent. I assume this means that 10 percent of the Pop-Tart is riboflavin. Maybe it's the red stuff in the middle. Anyway, I'm hoping riboflavin is a good thing; if it turns out that it's a *bad* thing, like "riboflavin" is the Latin word for "cock-roach pus," then I am definitely in trouble.

But the point is that I would not have this helpful nutritional information if I lived in some lawless for-eign country that does not have strict food-labeling laws, or carelessly allows dried plums to be mar-keted under the name "dried plums." And that is only *one* advantage of living in the United States. There are many more, but I am not going to go into them, because I have already almost forgotten my topic here, which is: If we want to avoid having an-other weird presidential election, we should kick Florida out of the union.

As long as South Florida is part of the United States, weird things are going to happen to the na-tion. Because South Florida is a nuclear generator of weirdness. For one thing, it's a swamp. The entire lower end of the state is about the same height above sea level as Dustin Hoffman. All the people are squeezed onto the coastlines on either side; in the middle is the Everglades, a vast expanse of oozing muck populated by a small tribe of casino-dwelling Native Americans and at least 300 billion mosqui-toes, many with the wingspan of a mature osprey.

This means that if you move to South Florida, you are settling down smack-dab in the ancient stomp-ing grounds of a teeming mass of swamp and marine life, which apparently was never notified that this area is now supposed to be zoned for humans.

The first thing I noticed when I moved to the Miami area in 1986 was that I had crabs on my lawn. At my previous residence, in Pennsylvania, I had dealt with crab *grass*, but in Miami, when I went outside in the morning to pick up the newspaper I was confronted by actual *crabs*, dozens of them, scuttling around. And these crabs were *hostile*. It was crab mating season, when the male crabs defend the females fiercely. I'd be half asleep, stumbling back into the house with the paper in my hand, and my path would suddenly be blocked by an irate male crab, lunging at my bare toes with his pincers to keep me from having sex with his woman.

"I don't want to have sex with your woman!" I'd yell at him, leaping backward. "Your woman is a *crab*!" But that only made him angrier, because deep in his heart[3] he knew it was true.

My neighborhood was also the world convention headquarters for the International Association of Big Hairy Spiders. They looked like severely mutated Yorkshire terriers that had developed extra legs and eyeballs, and they were all over the place, in every tree and bush, spinning trampoline-size webs that could stop an NFL fullback. It goes without saying that South Florida also had active populations of ticks, gnats, psychotic fire ants, and these scary huge mutant grasshoppers that could, without any special effects, be cast as major villains in *Jurassic Park III*.

---

[3]Or possibly hearts, depending on how crabs work.

On the amphibian and reptile front, South Florida is semi-infested with large, hideous toads that secrete a deadly venom, which means they feel free to saunter onto your patio and sit there for hours, looking insolent, as if they expect you to make them a cheeseburger. And everywhere you look, indoors and out, you see lizards, scampering around and engaging in acts of wanton lizard sex. Many a morning I've awakened to the sight of a lizard on the bedroom ceiling, hanging casually upside down via his suction feet, looking at me with an expression that says: "Perhaps, while you were snoring, I pooped in your mouth."

I personally have encountered only a few smallish alligators, but there are plenty around; Florida's alligator population is currently estimated at over a million.[4] Every now and then the newspapers carry stories about alligators chomping on people's dogs, or, on occasion, actual people. It is not at all unusual for a Floridian in a nice suburban neighborhood to walk out onto the patio and discover an alligator in the swimming pool.

Or a major snake. People down here routinely find huge members of the constrictor family in their pools, or lounging on their patios. These are, believe it or not, escaped *pets*. That's right: As if there weren't already enough local snakes, some Florida residents[5]

[4]I think they have their own member of Congress.

[5]Not to name names, but one of these residents is my good friend Carl Hiaasen, the legendary South Florida columnist and novelist, who keeps pet snakes. He feeds them rats, which he buys at the pet store (rat sales are big down here). "I have to stop on the way home and get some rats" is something you will actually hear Carl say.

choose to import, both legally and illegally,[6] immense carnivorous snakes,[7] which are always getting out of their cages, causing the owners to become very worried about what might happen . . . to the *snakes*.

"Her name is Midge," they'll tell reporters, referring to a seventeen-foot escaped python capable of consuming a water buffalo whole. "She hasn't eaten in days! She must be terrified!"

Some of these escaped snakes are later found, wrapped around a tree, or a lamppost, or a slow-moving citizen. But many of them are never found, which means they're still out there somewhere, slithering around and feeding on God knows what. Perhaps cougars. You may think I'm kidding, but a surprising number of Floridians keep large, predatory, extremely nonvegetarian jungle cats as pets. A while back, the commissioners of Pompano Beach were forced to consider an ordinance requiring residents to keep their pets on their property after, in the words of *The Miami Herald*, "a cougar escaped from a private home and briefly chased a small boy."

So you do not want to randomly wander onto a

---

[6]Reptile smuggling is a big business down here. In 1999, a man arriving from Barbados was detained at the Miami airport when officials noticed that his pants had some suspicious, wriggling bulges; he turned out to have *fifty-five turtles* in there. *The Miami Herald* account of this does not say whether the man was wearing a protective cup, but let us hope to God he was.

[7]True story from *The Miami Herald*: A Hollywood, Florida, fire-fighter was searching through a burning house when he found a ten-foot boa constrictor in distress. He bravely grabbed its head, and the snake coiled around his body. He walked briskly outside and returned the snake to its owner, who said: "Thanks, man, but there's two more in there."

residential Florida property. A painting contractor once told me that one of his men, while attempting to do a job, got chased out of a backyard by an extremely angry emu.

"He was on the radio, scared to death," the contractor said. "He was shouting 'THERE'S A GIANT CHICKEN IN THERE!' "

Did I mention the monkeys? When Hurricane Andrew hit South Florida in August of 1992, hundreds of monkeys and baboons escaped from residences and research facilities and roamed loose in southern Dade County. Two months after the hurricane, the state game commission reported that more than 450 escaped primates (not to mention more than two thousand escaped reptiles) were still at large. This total included fifty to one hundred baboons.

The game commission warned residents not to approach the primates; unfortunately, nobody was warning the primates not to approach the residents. One day shortly after the hurricane, I was waiting in my yard for a contractor, who arrived late in a pickup truck with one of his employees, both of them looking upset. They told me they'd been delayed by an irate baboon that jumped into the bed of the pickup and started pounding on the rear window so hard they thought it was going to break. The contractor, taking charge, told the employee to get out and scare the baboon away; the employee, not being an idiot, said to the contractor, "Hey, it's *your* truck, *you* get out there."

So they both wisely remained inside the truck and drove around randomly for a while, with the baboon pounding away on their window, a hitchhiker from hell. Finally it jumped out of the truck and they sped off, leaving the baboon shrieking and making obscene primate gestures at them.

You had to feel sorry for the baboon. During the post-Andrew chaos there was a widespread rumor, which turned out to be false, that the escaped baboons and monkeys had the AIDS virus. As a result, many of them were shot by South Florida residents, who own as many guns as the North Korean army, although ours are generally of a higher caliber.

People often ask me: Why do people down there have so many guns? The answer is: Shut up or I'll kill you.

No, seriously, South Floridians need guns for many valid reasons. For example, when South Floridians drive, they routinely fire their weapons at or near other motorists to convey important messages, such as "I would like you to get out of my way," or "I have a gun."

If you think I'm exaggerating, it's only because you never lived in South Florida. Since I moved here, I have personally seen two guns pulled in traffic, and at least a half-dozen cars with bullet holes in the driver's side. In other parts of the country, when you teach your child how to drive, you say things like: "This is a four-way stop, so you have the right-of-way over that man to your left." Here in South Florida, we tell our children, "Let that man go first, because he is brandishing his Glock."

Another reason why many South Floridians have guns is of course for self-protection. My personal favorite example of this is a Broward County case in which a lawyer named Frank Furci was walking

his Doberman pinscher, Ginger, through his affluent Broward County neighborhood, when he was
approached by another dog, named Claude. Furci
later claimed he thought Claude, an aging sheepdog, was attacking Ginger. This was disputed by the
person who was walking Claude, a woman named
Jan Bongers, who claimed that Claude was just being friendly and merely "waggled up to" Ginger.

In a normal place, the two dogs would have
fought, or sniffed each other's butts, or the two
owners might have separated them. Or perhaps
even the two owners would have sniffed each other's
butts. The one thing we know for sure is that, in a
normal place, what would *not* have happened is what
happened in this case, which is that Mr. Furci, a
lawyer in an affluent neighborhood, shot Claude the
sheepdog with a .45-caliber revolver. The reason he
was carrying a .45, he later said, was that his law firm
had received threats related to a recent case. There
was no indication whether any of these threats had
come from sheepdogs. But you can't be too careful.

Mr. Furci was charged with cruelty to animals and
aggravated assault. But there is more to this story.
(In South Florida, there is *always* more to the story.) It
happened that Mr. Furci's partner was Roy Black, the
well-known Miami defense attorney who later successfully defended William Kennedy Smith when
he was charged with rape in Palm Beach after going out drinking with national role model Edward M.
Kennedy.

Mr. Black put on what I would venture to guess
was the most elaborate courtroom defense ever
mounted on behalf of a person charged with shooting

a sheepdog. I quote here from a *Miami Herald* story, written by Neely Tucker:

> Aerial photographs of the scene were developed. An autopsy was ordered. Claude, who had been frozen, was thawed to room temperature. No less than Dr. Ronald K. Wright, Broward's chief medical examiner, handled the post-mortem. Eight by 10 glossies of Claude's jugular vein, ripped apart by the exploding bullet, were printed. X-rays were made. Bullet fragments were analyzed. Black filed 43 motions and took 17 depositions. In the end, Furci pleaded no contest to a cruelty to animals charge, paid $4,000 to charities and donated 50 hours to community service. Claude did not die in vain. As far as can be determined, not a single lawyer has since blown away a single sheepdog in Broward County.

But I digress.[8] The point I was making is that many South Florida residents feel the need to have guns for self-defense. But guns are also traditionally used down here for happy reasons. In parts of Miami, it is traditional to celebrate festive occasions—particularly New Year's Eve, but also July Fourth, Halloween, and sometimes just the fact that the sun has gone down—by getting drunk, going outside, and shooting guns into the air. On New Year's Eve, parts of Miami sound like a war zone, only louder. Unfortu-

---

[8]If you don't like digressions, you should get out of this chapter right now.

nately, the law of gravity—one of the few laws observed in Miami on New Year's Eve—causes many of the bullets to come back down, which is why police and firefighters do not venture into these areas until the rain of lead is over.

But we do not use our guns only on joyful occasions. In 1997, in Little Havana, a gun battle, involving semiautomatic weapons, broke out *in a funeral home, during a wake.*

At this point you are wondering: Do South Floridians ever use their guns to fight crime? They surely do. I know this because of the following true anecdote that was told to me by a friend of mine named Penny Gardner, who used to operate a VIP hosting service. Several years ago, she went to Miami International Airport to pick up Cleveland Amory, a distinguished author who had come to South Florida to promote a book.

Penny had rented a large car for Amory. She ushered him into the passenger seat, and she had just opened the driver's-side door when a man came sprinting up, grabbed her purse, and leaped into a getaway car, which raced off with Penny running after it.

So far this is a normal anecdote, the kind of thing that could happen in front of a distinguished visiting author in any big city. But what happened next, I contend, would happen only in Miami: A passing motorist, having seen the crime, stopped his car in the middle of the street, leaped out, pulled out a gun, and started *shooting at the fleeing car.* He fired four or five shots, all of which apparently missed. Then, without a word to Penny, he got back into his car and drove off. The Good Miami Samaritan.

Penny, seriously shaken, rushed over to the rental-car agency, whose employees, in heartwarming we're-all-in-this-together South Florida fashion, had locked the door and were informing her, through the glass, that this incident had *not* occurred on their property. Meanwhile, distinguished author Cleveland Amory was lying sideways on the car seat, possibly wondering if this was, in fact, the kind of community where people purchase a lot of books. Welcome to Miami, sir! Anything we can do to make your stay more comfortable? Bulletproof vest? Change of underwear?

When you live here, you eventually get used to the fact that a certain amount of criminal activity is always going to be part of the environment, like palm trees, or retired ladies who think their hair looks natural dyed the same tint of red as a fire truck. I was once about to enter a Burger King on Biscayne Boulevard in downtown Miami when a man holding a gun came racing out, knocked down a pedestrian, jumped into a car, and drove wildly out of the parking lot, barely missing me and several other people.

Going into Junior Crimestopper mode, I alertly observed the car's license plate number and then raced into the restaurant, prepared to find a scene of shock and panic. Instead I found that the customers had calmly resumed chewing their Whoppers. I went up to an employee behind the counter, who told me that yes, there had been a robbery, but it had been reported. He was not interested in writing down my clue. Ho-hum, another armed robbery.

In the first neighborhood where I lived down here—a nice, upscale area—the large house at the end of the street was occupied by drug dealers.

That's what all the neighbors said, and I believed them, because the people who lived in the house never seemed to do anything to support themselves except wash their own cars, and there was a stream of unfriendly, secretive people entering and leaving the house at all hours.

This was viewed, in the neighborhood, as vaguely noteworthy, but not particularly uncommon; the house was simply another neighborhood landmark—the Liebmans' house, the Williamses' house, the Drug Dealers' house, etc. My son would ask if he could ride his bike, and I, being a responsible South Florida parent, would say, "OK, but don't go beyond the Drug Dealers' house!"

Once I was having a beer at the bar of a small restaurant on Miami Beach, and a man recognized me from my picture in the newspaper. Here, without embellishment, is how our conversation went:

MAN: You the one who write for the newspaper?
ME: Yes.
MAN: You should write about Colombia! A lot of humor there! You ever been to Colombia?
ME: No.
MAN: Hah! I am from there. Let me be honest. I am a narcotics trafficker.

I swear that's exactly what he said. There were two police officers eating dinner maybe ten feet away, and he said "I am a narcotics trafficker" in the same open, friendly voice you might use to say "I am a claims adjuster." I half expected him to give me his business card.

The drug trade is definitely part of the economy down here. Law-enforcement agents are always seizing heroin and cocaine shipments the size of major geological formations; these stories are so routine they almost never make the front page. Occasionally, tourists walking along the beach encounter bales of marijuana or cocaine—sometimes worth millions—that washed ashore after being tossed overboard by smugglers fleeing the Coast Guard. This kind of thing probably happens more often than is reported to the police. ("Where are the kids, dear?" "They're at the beach again." "But it's raining!" "I know! They *really* love that beach!")[9]

Down here, drugs turn up in the *darnedest* places. In 1999, dozens of workers at Miami International Airport[10] were charged with smuggling guns, hand grenades, and drugs onto passenger jets. One of the hiding places used for the drugs was in the airplane coffee filters; this was discovered when—I swear I am not making this up—a pilot was mistakenly served *coffee laced with heroin*. Fortunately the pilot realized something was wrong with the coffee and did not drink it; otherwise, God only knows what kind of flight it would have been. ("This is the captain speaking. We're gonna see if this baby can do a loop.")

[9]Not everything that washes up on the beach is fun. In 1995, beachgoers in four places over a three-mile stretch of shoreline found a pelvis, right leg, upper arm, shoulder, collarbone, lower jaw, and spinal column that police identified as belonging to a man named Aniello Napolitano III. *The Miami Herald* gave his occupation as "bodyguard."

[10]I will not go into detail on Miami International Airport, except to say that if you go there, there's no need for you to visit the Third World.

But even that is not the best example of a South Florida Unexpected Drug Encounter. That distinction, in my opinion, belongs to the surreal July evening in 1992 when a neighborhood Crime Watch group held its first meeting out on the patio of a nice house in a nice suburban neighborhood of the city of Homestead.

The Homestead chief of police, a man named Curt Ivy, was addressing the group, talking about the kinds of things the citizens should be on the lookout for, the clues that might indicate possible criminal activity. Chief Ivy was saying that it was a pretty quiet area, with not much illegal activity. But the chief was having trouble making his point, because of the engine noise from a low-flying plane.

"So I look up," Ivy later told me, "and this plane is coming, and it's low. It's very low. Then I see a package come sailing down."

The package, as you have surely guessed by now, was: the frozen body of Claude the sheepdog.

No, seriously, it was a seventy-five-pound cocaine bale. That's correct: *A bale of cocaine fell from the sky onto a Crime Watch meeting.* This was one of an estimated twenty cocaine bales, weighing a total of half a ton, that were frantically shoved out of a twin-engine plane being pursued by a U.S. Customs jet. Another bale narrowly missed a church and slammed into a car. Imagine trying to explain *that* to your insurance agent. ("Were drugs involved in this accident?" "Well . . .")

This was not the first instance of drugs falling from the South Florida skies. In 1981, a man was sleeping on a sofa in a Broward County trailer, and he got up to go to the bathroom. This was very fortunate, because moments later, a hundred-pound bale of marijuana came crashing through the roof of the room he had just left.

"If I had stayed where I was," the man said, "I would have been wiped out."

So in South Florida, it is not always enough to "just say no" to drugs. You may also need a bomb shelter.

My point is that there is a lot of drug trafficking down here, duh. Naturally you are wondering what we, as a community, have done about it. Here's one thing we did: *We named a street after a major drug dealer*. I am serious. Dade County commissioners—who are always naming streets after themselves, their friends, their dogs, etc.—named a section of West 132nd Avenue the "Leomar Parkway" in honor of Leonel Martinez, who had gone very rapidly from being the debt-ridden owner of a small, struggling garment business to being a wealthy developer. In addition to naming a street after Martinez, Dade County issued a proclamation citing his "fantastic accomplishments."

A few months later, law-enforcement authorities announced that the key to Mr. Martinez's fantastic accomplishments was that he was, um, running a large narcotics operation. As you can imagine, everybody was shocked, shocked. In response, the commissioners took harsh punitive action: *They changed the name of the street back to 132nd Avenue*. This bold move was proposed by then-commissioner Larry Hawkins, who, in one of my all-time favorite South Florida quotations, had this to say about "Leomar

Parkway": "I think it sends the wrong message, not only to kids in our community, but to drug dealers."

Damn straight it does! Let this story serve as a chilling warning to anybody who thinks he can get away with dealing drugs in South Florida: If you get caught, mister, *we will take your name off your street*.

Sometimes we take even harsher measures against alleged drug dealers. Sometimes we actually arrest and prosecute them in court. Unfortunately, since these courts are located in South Florida, things do not always turn out the way the forces of law and order had hoped. For an excellent example of this, let us consider the legendary case of Augusto "Willie" Falcon and Salvador "Sal" Magluta, or, as they are known in Miami, Willie and Sal.

Willie and Sal were offshore powerboat racers who were charged by the federal government with smuggling into the United States seventy-five tons of cocaine, worth $2.1 billion. Yes, you read that correctly: *seventy-five tons* of cocaine. To give you an idea how much cocaine that is: It would meet the needs of an NBA team for nearly a *week*.

No, all kidding aside, that is a *lot* of cocaine. The feds thought they had a pretty good case, even though two of their potential witnesses were unable to testify because somebody—and I am not for one second suggesting that this is anything other than sheer coincidence—murdered them.

In their Miami trial, Willie and Sal were defended by a team of big-name, high-priced lawyers. The defense allowed as how, OK, maybe at one time Willie and Sal dabbled in the drug trade, but that was *years* earlier, and they had retired. The feds argued, among other things, that Willie and Sal were still living very high on the hog, with millions of dollars' worth of real estate, plus their powerboat-racing team, and that they probably were not paying for this lifestyle by doing yard work.

One of the defense lawyers, it goes without saying, was Roy Black, of Claude-the-Attack-Sheepdog fame. In his closing remarks, Black—and this is the kind of classy defense you get when you pay millions of dollars—not only invoked Robert F. Kennedy and Martin Luther King, Jr., but also quoted the eighteenth-century English statesman Edmund Burke as saying: "The only thing necessary for the triumph of evil is for good men to do nothing." (For the record, most scholars believe that when Burke said this, he most likely was not specifically referring to either Willie or Sal.)

Nevertheless, the consensus was that the feds, who produced tons of witnesses, had nailed Willie and Sal good. So everybody was *very* surprised when the jury came back and acquitted them of all charges.

The feds were stunned. As U.S. attorney Kendall Coffey put it: "Certainly, this is a dark moment for us."

Coffey was not just whistling Dixie. He really was depressed. And so he did what so many of us do to pick ourselves up when we're feeling down in the dumps: He went to a strip bar called "Lipstik," bought a $900 bottle of Dom Perignon champagne, and bit a topless dancer on the arm. That is correct: *South Florida's top federal law enforcement official bit a stripper.* She was a former head bank teller who danced under the name of "Tiffany," although her actual name was "Tammy." (I realize that you think I'm making this up, but trust me, my imagination is nowhere *near* creative enough to come up with stuff this good.)

When word of this incident got out, Coffey announced his resignation (to his everlasting credit, he did not drag Edmund Burke into it). But of course that was not the end of the story (as I mentioned earlier, in South Florida, the story *never* ends). Coffey went into private practice and ended up being a member of the legal team representing the Miami relatives of Elián Gonzalez, the little boy who, for a while, served as the rope in the ongoing insane tug-of-war between the United States and Cuba (more on this later). After losing that particular fight, Coffey became a major part of the legal team fighting for Al Gore in the Florida presidential-recount battle, which as you may recall (although I doubt it) is the subject of this chapter.

But getting back to Willie and Sal: As I said, everybody was stunned when they were acquitted by the jury on all charges. See if you can guess the next major legal development in this case.

If you said: "The jury foreman was convicted of taking nearly half a million dollars in bribes to throw the verdict," then you are definitely getting the hang of South Florida. (In case you were wondering: Yes, the jury foreman worked at Miami International Airport.)

The feds suspected that the bribes and at least some of the $25 million that Willie and Sal and their codefendants paid to defense lawyers came from— prepare to be astonished—the sale of illegal narcotics. Eventually, the government brought bribery and money-laundering charges against some alleged members of the Willie and Sal operation. (One of these was a guy who was making $43,000 a year as a refrigerator mechanic with the Miami-Dade County school district; he apparently was very frugal, because agents found $6 million *cash in his attic*.)

As you can imagine, the defense lawyers were extremely indignant about the suggestion that they should have suspected that drugs had anything to do with the millions of dollars, much of it in cash, that they were paid by alleged drug dealers. They strongly criticized the government's efforts to trace the source of their legal fees ("We're halfway to fascism," said Roy Black).

The resulting legal proceedings produced a fascinating look into the financial dealings of big-time South Florida defense lawyers. Frank Rubino,[11] who represented a codefendant of Willie and Sal, testified that he received eight payments of $50,000 in cash from a man he knew only as "Baldy." Rubino said he did not see a problem with this, because his client told him that "the money was from a legitimate source of income."

Makes sense to me! I know that whenever a guy whom I know only as "Baldy" regularly gives *me* $50,000 in cash, my immediate and natural reaction is: "Well *this* is surely from a legitimate source of income!"

---

[11]Rubino also represented former Panamanian dictator Manuel Noriega when Noriega was tried in Miami on drug and racketeering charges. I feel compelled to note here that during that trial, Noriega's wife, Felicidad, was arrested in an upscale Dade County department store on shoplifting charges after she—*the former first lady of Panama*—was seen snipping buttons off ladies' jackets.

Attorney Ed Shohat, who also represented a Willie-and-Sal codefendant, testified that one day a man he did not know came into his office, dropped a briefcase containing $150,000 cash on the floor, and *ran out*.

Now, to me, this does not seem at *all* suspicious. Hardly a day goes by when somebody doesn't drop a briefcase containing a very large quantity of cash on my floor and sprint from the room. But attorney Shohat was concerned enough about the source of this money that he took the precaution of checking with his client to make sure it was legit. Shohat testified that his client "assured me after several discussions that the source of the funds was a loan to him from people unrelated to Sal Magluta and Willie Falcon." Well OK, then! That clears *that* up!

I could go on and on about the Willie and Sal case, which itself is still going on and on as I write these words. Perhaps someday, when it's all over, it will be made into a great comedy movie, starring Jim Carrey as both Willie and Sal, with Jennifer Lopez as the topless dancer who gets bitten on the arm, and Keanu Reeves as Claude the sheepdog.

But I want to move on here, because I don't want you to get the impression that South Florida is just a bunch of criminals who run drugs. Not true! Some of them also run our government.

I am not saying that every South Florida politician is corrupt. Some are merely insane. As I write these words, the popular nicknames for the current and previous mayors of the city of Miami are, respectively, "Crazy Joe" and "Mayor Loco."

"Crazy Joe," the current mayor, is Joe Carollo, who got his nickname from the fact that he is known to have quite a temper, and he generally has the facial expression of a very tightly wound, possibly paranoid person whose head is filled with small but very violent animals—ferrets, maybe—that at any moment are going to explode out of his skull directly through his eyeballs and attack you.

"Mayor Loco" was the nickname given to Crazy Joe's political archenemy, Xavier Suarez. He was widely considered to be sane when he defeated Crazy Joe in the 1997 mayoral election, but this perception changed almost immediately when Mayor Loco took office and began behaving as though he were (to put it in technical psychological terms) a few forks short of a fondue set.

For one thing, Mayor Loco went around loudly insisting that Miami did not have a financial crisis, when it was a well-established fact that the city was way beyond flat broke, thanks to years of being run by politicians who have consistently displayed a degree of fiscal prudence and foresight rarely seen except among crack addicts.

But the big reason why Mayor Loco was nicknamed "Mayor Loco" was that he tended to be, as the newspapers put it, "erratic." For example, when Mayor Loco got a critical letter from a Miami resident named Edna Benson, the mayor decided to respond by personally visiting her house, unannounced, at 10:30 P.M., on a weekday. Mrs. Benson, a retired city employee, was home alone, with her hair in curlers, when she heard the doorbell ring. Now that you're familiar with life in South Florida, see if you can guess what happened next. Here are two scenarios:

Scenario One: Mrs. Benson and the mayor talked, and, after hearing his side of the story, she changed her mind.

Scenario Two: Mrs. Benson and the mayor talked, and although she appreciated hearing his point of view, in the end she still disagreed with his actions.

If you think Scenario One is correct, you are wrong. This is also true if you think Scenario Two is correct. The correct, only-in-Miami answer is:

Scenario Three: Mrs. Benson picked up her five-shot, .38-caliber revolver ("It's got those bullets that do damage," she later told *The Miami Herald*). Then she went to the window and peeked out, fearing that there was a burglar outside. When she saw that it was in fact the mayor—the city's highest official— she naturally . . . *refused to open the door.*

"He looked mad," she said, "really, really mad."
I should tell you that one of the reasons Mrs. Benson criticized Mayor Loco in her letter was that he had appointed a Miami city commissioner named Humberto Hernandez to be chairman of the commission. What made this appointment slightly questionable, to Mrs. Benson and other observers, was that at the time, Hernandez was awaiting trial on charges of bank fraud and money laundering.
The fact that Hernandez was under indictment

had not prevented him from being overwhelmingly reelected to the Miami City Commission by his constituents. The simple truth is that, in South Florida, being indicted almost guarantees that a candidate will win an election race; the voters seem to view it as a plus, proof that you understand how the political system works.

The best example of this is the mayor of Hialeah, Raul Martinez, who was indicted, and then convicted, on federal racketeering and extortion charges in connection with a ballot-tampering case. This did not prevent the voters from returning him to office *twice*, in landslide victories, while he appealed. Ultimately, he won the appeal, but you will not find a soul down here who does not believe that he would have continued to be reelected even if he had lost.

But getting back to Humberto Hernandez, the indicted man appointed by Mayor Loco to head the Miami City Commission: He ended up pleading guilty in the bank fraud case, although things got a little sticky on the legal ethics front when it was discovered that his lawyer, José Quinon (who, for the record, also had represented Hialeah mayor Martinez) had been having an affair with Hernandez's wife while Hernandez was in jail. Now, follow me closely here, because it gets complicated: At this point, Hernandez was *not* in jail for the bank fraud case. He was in jail after being convicted on *another* charge, namely, helping to cover up vote fraud in the election that put Mayor Loco in office.

As it turned out, that election featured a *lot* of vote fraud, even by Miami standards. *The Miami Herald* won a Pulitzer Prize for an investigation proving that many of the ballots cast in the Miami city election were cast by people who did not, if you wanted to get picky about it, reside in Miami. The *Herald* contacted some of these people, who gave some truly wonderful, even heartwarming, explanations, including these, which I am not making up:

- *A woman who had moved out of Miami but continued to vote in city elections for thirteen years:* "I know I shouldn't be doing it. But I don't want to forget my people, my blood."
- *Members of a family that lived outside of Miami, but drove as a group to the city and voted every election day:* "It's a tradition." And: "The important things, we do as a family together."
- *The wife in a couple who had moved out of Miami but continued to vote there:* "When we moved, I couldn't vote for the people I liked here."
- *A man who had moved to Hialeah, but continued to vote in Miami:* "I've always felt more in tune with things in Miami than anywhere else. Look, I'm an American citizen and I feel you don't violate the law when you vote. It's my right as an American citizen."

Damn right! This is America, where a person has the fundamental right to vote in the municipality of his choosing, regardless of where he lives!

I do not mean to suggest, by the previous statement, that to vote in Miami you absolutely have to meet the rigid and arbitrary standard of being alive. The *Herald* found that a vote had been cast in the 1997 Miami election by a Mr. Manuel Yip, who passed away in 1993. In fact, since his burial, Mr. Yip had voted in *at least six elections*. Talk about exercising your rights as an American!

Anyway, when all this vote fraud stuff started coming out, former mayor Crazy Joe went to court to challenge his loss to Mayor Loco. See if you can guess which lawyer represented Crazy Joe in this case.

If you guessed "former U.S. attorney Kendall Coffey, the guy who bit the topless dancer on the arm and also represented both Elián Gonzalez and Al Gore," then you are really getting the hang of South Florida.

In the end, the courts kicked Mayor Loco out of office, and put Crazy Joe back in charge of the city of Miami. As I write these words, ex-Mayor Loco is gearing up to run for mayor again. Crazy Joe was making some moves in that direction himself, but then he got arrested, and spent a night in jail, after allegedly bopping his wife on the head with a cardboard tea box. So it is not clear what lies ahead for these two men, but I sincerely hope that they remain on the public scene, after all the years of quality entertainment they have provided. Plus, what's the big deal about mayors acting a little crazy? It's not as if they tried to kill somebody!

Which is more than you can say for the ex-mayor of Hialeah Gardens, a woman named Gilda Oliveros, also known, because of the way she dressed, as the "Miniskirt Mayor." She was arrested on charges of soliciting two city employees[12] in 1996 and 1997 to

---

[12]My feeling about this is, even if she did it, she should have been found not guilty, because anybody who asks municipal employees to perform a task would know that it would never actually get done.

murder her then-husband so she could collect on a life-insurance policy. (I assume it goes without saying that she was also charged with vote fraud.)

The Miniskirt Mayor denied the charges. "I have good legs," she said. "I'm tall. I'm good-looking. And yes, I explode easily. I scream for five minutes, but then I get over it. I'm certainly not going to kill anyone."

Oliveros went on trial in 1999. I'm sure that by now you've guessed that the attorney who represented her was none other than: Ed Shohat, recipient of the totally nonsuspicious briefcase containing $150,000 in completely legitimate cash.

The trial featured allegations by the prosecution that Oliveros was having an affair with the former mayor of Hialeah, Julio Martinez (not to be confused with the *current* mayor of Hialeah, Raul Martinez, the one who got reelected twice while he was appealing his conviction on racketeering and extortion charges). The defense suggested that the main witnesses against the Miniskirt Mayor were gay lovers who were setting the mayor up because they had an ax to grind.

Nevertheless, the Miniskirt Mayor was convicted and sentenced to four years in prison. I am confident that she will have no trouble resuming her political career when she gets out, or maybe even before.

I have, in this chapter, discussed only a few of the many South Florida politicians, judges, and civil servants, of all ethnic groups and genders, who were convicted of one crime or another and still somehow managed to wind up rich and respected in our generous and forgiving community. That's the kind of "live and let live" place South Florida is.

   This generous spirit is not new. It's why Al Capone
chose to live here, as did Meyer Lansky, as did
Richard Nixon. And needless to say, when O. J. Simpson decided to move to a place where he would fit
right in, he chose South Florida. Everyone is welcome!

This brings us to the melting-pot aspect of South
Florida. If ever there was a bunch of people melting
inside a pot, this is it. Among the major groups attempting to coexist down here are:

Natives: These are the roughly twenty-seven people
who were born and raised in South Florida and are
still here. They are always telling you how great it
used to be down here before people like you came
and ruined it—how there used to be no traffic, no
crime, steady breezes, friendly pacifist/vegan mos-
quitoes, free beer, flamingos strolling on Biscayne
Boulevard, and large succulent fish that jumped voluntarily out of the ocean right onto your barbecue. It
was heaven! A lot of these people have skin lesions.

Retirees: These are the people who moved down
here after they stopped working (or, in some cases,
died) so they could relax, play bingo, wear their
pants really high, eat dinner at 4:30 P.M., and drive
their 1987 Oldsmobiles at a constant, unvarying
speed of twenty-three miles an hour everywhere, including through red lights, on the interstate, and on
sidewalks. Sometimes they drive into buildings, but
this is not really their fault, inasmuch as they cannot
see the buildings. Retirees tend to clump together in

large condominiums, where they while away their golden years accusing one another of violating the rules.

New Yorkers: There seem to be millions of them down here, and I frankly don't know why they stay, because they're always pointing out, in voices that can be clearly heard on other planets, how much better New York is. Listening to them talk about New York's infinitely superior neighborhoods, culture, sports fans, Chinese food, etc., you get the impression that New York is some kind of urban paradise, instead of an expensive, crowded, grimy place that always smells faintly of pee.

Ohioans: I am using "Ohioans" generically here, to represent people from normal parts of the country (by which I mean all parts other than New York) who get transferred to the Miami area and are quickly stunned into a state of stark quivering terror by the huge bugs and the psychotic drivers and the four billion percent humidity and the general permeating weirdness. The Ohioans who stay generally move to Broward County and huddle together in identical houses inside gated developments wishfully named for geographic elements that do not exist in South Florida, as in Oak Manour Estates at the Meadows of the Falls Phase IV.

French-Canadians: They come down in large numbers for the winter months and are a positive force for unity in South Florida, in the sense that all the other groups down here, which do not agree on anything else, hate them, because they drive even worse than the retirees and their idea of a good tip is 3 percent.[13]

European Tourists: Many Europeans vacation in South Florida, especially Miami Beach, which they like because it has a relaxed ambience of cosmopolitan sophistication, by which I mean it's OK to be pretty much naked. American tourists are often stunned when they go to the beach and see European women flagrantly displaying their bosoms. This phenomenon often causes American men, who are trying to look as casual as possible while maintaining eye contact at all times with the European women's nipples, to walk directly into the lifeguard tower. The downside of the European sophistication is that many European men, even if they are as large and hairy as water buffalo, insist on wearing pouch-style bathing suits the size of eye patches, thus transforming the beach into the traditional European Festival of the Hairy Buttcracks.

Immigrants: Outsiders tend to lump these all together under the label "Cubans." There *are* a lot of Cubans, and they dominate Miami, economically and politically. But there are also large numbers of immigrants from elsewhere in the Caribbean and Central and South America—so many that Miami sometimes feels, especially if you just got here from Ohio, like a foreign country. There are large areas in Miami where you will hear people speaking only

[13] I'm just kidding, of course. It's more like 2 percent.

Spanish, or Creole. I have seen signs in store windows that say ENGLISH SPOKEN HERE.[14]

Me, I like this international flavor. Of course, my wife is of Cuban descent, which has made it easier for me. For example, I now speak Spanish fluently. I don't mean that I can speak the whole entire Spanish *language*; I mean that I have learned to say, with great fluency, the following phrase: "Un momento; mi esposa habla español" ("One moment; my wife speaks Spanish"). My wife takes over from there.[15]

Still, the language thing is sometimes a problem for me. When I'm with my wife's family, everybody, for my sake, speaks English; but sometimes, to make a point, somebody will use an old traditional Cuban folk saying, of which there seem to be thousands. Then they'll translate it for me, and it'll be something like, "You don't need three elbows to play the flute," or "The dog that drives a tractor can laugh at the snake." And I'll nod thoughtfully, while thinking, Huh?

I have also had to adjust to the Latin concept of time, which over the years has been the biggest single source of friction between my wife and me. I believe in what I will call the Anglo Theory of time,

[14]True story: My wife and her mother were at a Julio Iglesias concert in Miami, and Julio, who usually sings in Spanish, started a song in English. This prompted the man sitting next to my wife to say to his wife (in Spanish): "He should sing in Spanish! This is Miami! If he wants to sing in English, he should go to Minneapolis!"
[15]The other Spanish sentence that I have learned to say fluently is: "Mientras sus zapatos se estiran, yo bailaría el mambo contigo." ("While your shoes are stretching, I will dance the mambo with you.") You'd be *amazed* how useful this is.

which holds that there is only so much time in a day—roughly, twenty-four hours. Consequently, if you sincerely intend to accomplish a specific task in a given day—say, get to the airport—then at some point during that day you must actually take concrete steps in the direction of getting to the airport, lest you run out of time.

My wife's theory—the Latin Theory—holds that each day contains an infinite amount of time; thus, there is never any need to do anything *now*. My wife believes she can do *everything* later. As a result, she tends to run late, at least from my Anglo perspective. Of course from *her* perspective, she is never running late, because there is an infinite amount of time ahead.

Miami, being predominantly Latin, operates mostly under my wife's theory of time. So if you're an Anglo down here, you must learn to interpret what people really mean when they use certain time-related expressions. Here's a chart to help you:

EXPRESSION	ANGLO MEANING	LATIN MEANING
"Right now"	Immediately	Later
"Today"	At some point in the current day	Maybe tomorrow. But maybe not.
"Tomorrow"	The day following today	Maybe next week. Definitely not tomorrow.
"Later"	At some future point	Probably never
"At 7 P.M."	Roughly at 7 P.M.	This has no Latin meaning

The other major Anglo-Latin difference I have noticed involves levels of passion. As a group, Latins have a *much* higher passion quotient than Anglos. At public events in Miami, if there's music playing, you can easily distinguish between the two groups, because the Anglos will not be responding to the music at all, except maybe to tap their styluses on their Palm Pilots in a slightly more rhythmic manner. Whereas the Latins will be *dancing.* And I mean *all* the Latins—young Latins, old Latins, dogs belonging to Latins—they will *all* be swiveling their hips, even if those hips are artificial.

Fact: *The average Anglo moves his hips less during his entire lifetime than the average Latin moves his hips during a single performance of the national anthem.*

To me, the Latin passion is one of the best things about life in Miami, where people tend to respond to almost every occasion—birthdays, weddings, anniversaries, successful dental procedures—by throwing parties that can last for days. I love this aspect of Miami, the Latin energy that infuses it and vitalizes it, and is largely responsible for building it into a great city.

But sometimes the passion gets out of hand. This is particularly true in the area of Miami politics, by which I basically mean Cuban politics. For much of Miami, Cuba remains *the* issue; we are the only large American city I know of that has its own foreign policy. Fidel Castro is, by far, the most influential politician in Miami, in the sense that much of the political debate here consists of politicians screaming at one another about who hates Fidel the most.

Let me stress that I find this totally understandable. Castro is an evil egomaniac who has, through repression, brutality, theft, and murder, blighted a nation and its people. I don't think any person with a brain doubts this; anybody who *does* can come to Miami and talk to the many Cuban Americans—my in-laws, for example—who had all their property taken by Castro's thugs, or whose family members lost their liberty, or their lives, for daring to dissent.

To Cuban Americans, what Castro is, and why he should be despised, is obvious; it frustrates and infuriates them when outsiders fail to see it. Every few months, it seems, some celebrity twit visits Cuba, gets escorted around by government toadies, and is wined and dined and charmed by Castro (who can be very charming). And then this twit, having met not one ordinary Cuban citizen, and knowing nothing about Cuban history or about real life on the island, makes some astoundingly twittish pronouncement. In 1998, for example, Naomi Campbell visited Cuba and declared, based on her extensive training as a supermodel, that Castro was "a source of inspiration to the world."

Around the same time, noted human-rights authority Jack Nicholson described Castro as "a genius." Describing his visit with Castro, Nicholson said: "We spoke about everything. It was plain old talk. We talked about life, culture. . . . He stays up late, like me."

Well, OK, then! What could possibly be wrong with a guy who *stays up late*, like Jack?

This kind of idiot statement—while people are still regularly dying on rafts in their efforts to escape Cuba—causes even my wife, who is normally pretty laid-back, to say bad words. It makes the harder-core Miami Cubans absolutely nuts. I'm talking about the older Cubans, the ones who once fought Castro, the ones who think of themselves as exiles, because they dream of going back and retaking their island from the bearded Satan.

Of course they won't: Castro won, and they lost. That is the permanent salt in the permanent wound that is Miami's exile community. Castro is in Havana, and they're in Miami. It is almost impossible for outsiders to understand how angry, how bitter, how frustrated this makes the exiles. That anger constantly bubbles just below the surface in Miami.

Over the years, this anger has often erupted into outright craziness. Some of this is scary craziness. There was a period, lasting until not that long ago, when heavily armed paramilitary outfits regularly trained in the Everglades, and members of rival exile groups were assassinated, and bombs blew up outside Miami businesses and organizations deemed to be not anti-Castro enough.

But a lot of the anti-Castro craziness is more along the lines of wacky. Take the legendary case of Orlando Bosch, a former pediatrician and revered anti-Castro zealot who over the years was linked to an impressive array of bombings, raids, and assassination plots. In 1964, Bosch was arrested for driving in downtown Miami rush-hour traffic—*towing a torpedo*. In 1968 Bosch, striking a blow against communism, stood on the MacArthur Causeway and *fired a bazooka* at a Polish freighter docked in the port of Miami. (The freighter failed to sink, but it should be noted that, just twenty-three years later, the Soviet Union collapsed.)

There's less outright violence now, but the frustration is still here, bubbling, bubbling, and it still occasionally erupts in bizarre ways. To pick just a few fairly recent examples:

- In 1995, several dozen Cuban exiles formed a protest flotilla of pleasure boats that motored into Cuban waters. Two Cuban gunboats sideswiped the lead boat, causing a Miami-Dade County commissioner named Pedro Reboredo to lose his balance and get his foot smushed between boats. He was airlifted back to Miami, where doctors amputated the second toe on his right foot. Leaving the hospital, Reboredo said: "I couldn't be happier. It is very sweet to be able to give something for the country." This kind of thing does not happen to county commissioners in Iowa.
- In 1999, a Miami-Dade aviation official ordered the magazine *Cigar Aficionado* removed from the shelves of airport newsstands because it contained an article about Cuba that the official considered too positive. (*What* First Amendment? This is Miami!)
- On New Year's Day, 2000, exiles cheered when a fifty-one-year-old Vietnamese anticommunist named Ly Tong—who once hijacked an Air Vietnam flight over Ho Chi Minh City and dropped anticommunist leaflets from the cockpit—took off from Key West in a rented plane and flew to Havana, where he circled the city, dropping leaflets calling for rebellion and describing Fidel as "an old dinosaur." For this bold strike against tyranny, Tong was honored as a hero in a Little Havana parade and awarded a medal by an anti-Castro group.

Of course the best-publicized recent example of Miami's anti-Castro obsession was the Elián Gonzalez fiasco. To Anglos, this appeared to be a straightforward case: A boy's mother died, so he should be with his father. But to the Miami exiles, it was not really about the family. It was about what everything is always about in Miami: Fidel. If Fidel says the boy must go back, then *the boy must not go back*.

And so it turned into a crazy international carnival, replete with farcical sideshows—the Miami relatives, the advisers, the lawyers, the media hordes, the shouting street mobs, the "fisherman" who wasn't a fisherman, the tales of magical anti-Castro lifesaving dolphins, and the Virgin Mary appearing in a mirror.

The world saw this, and it concluded that Miami is insane. Which it is, no question. Totally insane. I'm just saying, there's a *reason*.

If you don't live in South Florida, you probably find this all laughable. That wacky Miami! Those crazy, torpedo-towing, bazooka-shooting, toe-losing Cubans! Perhaps you think none of this has any effect on you, up there in Ohio.

If that's what you think, perhaps you should consider this: The Elián case left the Miami Cubans *really* pissed off at the Clinton administration for sending Elián back to Satan. People down here believe—and for what it's worth, I think they're right—that this anger cost Al Gore a lot of Hispanic votes. In other words, without Elián, Al Gore would have easily won Florida, and thus the presidency.[16]

---

[16]This is not the first time that anti-Castro Miamians have affected the presidency. Remember Watergate?

So, Mr. or Mrs. Ohio Resident, it seems that the laugh is on you, ha ha! Because it was these wacky Miamians, plus a bunch of people in Palm Beach who cannot figure out how to punch a hole in a piece of cardboard, who decided who *your president* is!

Which brings us, full circle, back to the original topic of this chapter, which is: Fruit Flies of the Ryuku Islands.

No, really, it brings us back to the 2000 presidential election mess, and what practical steps we can take to prevent it from happening again. The point of this chapter, so far, has been to demonstrate that South Florida is one of the weirdest places in the nation, and that as long as we *keep* it in the nation, we are running the risk that our national political process will be infected by this weirdness.

I have several more, equally practical, suggestions for improving our election system, but this chapter has already gone on *way* too long. So I'll continue this discussion in the next chapter. But first, let's take just a moment to consider this:

CHAPTER EIGHT

The Making of the President 2000, Continued (or)

Quick!
Fetch Mr. Rather's
Tranquilizer Dart!
(or)
Lawyers
Out the Wazoo

IN THE LAST CHAPTER, I made the case that, as a nation, we can avoid embarrassing ourselves the way we did in the 2000 election by taking the simple step of kicking Florida, or at least South Florida, out of the union, and giving its electoral votes to some clout-deprived state such as North Dakota.[1] In this chapter, I want to talk about three other elements that played a huge role in screwing up the 2000 election, and that definitely need to be corrected. Those three elements are:

1. Television
2. Lawyers
3. Lawyers on television

[1] I'm assuming North Dakota is a state.

We'll start with television. If you stayed up all night on Election Night 2000, watching the major networks, with their million-dollar anchor studs and their expert commentators and their research staffs and their elaborate graphics and their exit polls and their computers, at some point—probably around seven the next morning—a thought occurred to you: *You would have been just as well-informed about the outcome of this election if you had spent the entire night watching your toaster.*

In fact, you would have been *better* informed. Because there is no way that one toaster, working alone, could possibly have misinformed you as thoroughly as the TV networks did. In case you've blocked that night out of your memory, let's review what Election Night 2000 looked like on TV to the average viewer with a remote control:

REMOTE CONTROL: CLICK
TOM BROKAW: If you're just joining us, NBC News is now predicting that Minnesota is definitely leaning toward Al Gore, with Arizona and South Carolina leaning toward George W. Bush, while Oregon, Delaware, and Idaho, as NBC News predicted earlier, remain in the category of "States with Three-Syllable Names." To find out the significance of all this, we go to our expert political analyst, Tim Russert, who is standing by with an eraser board in his hand and an estimated seventy-eight thousand milligrams of caffeine in his bloodstream. Tim, what does this mean?
TIM RUSSERT: Well, Tom, it could mean several things. On the one hand, if Minnesota stays with Gore,

and he is able to pick up either Vermont or Tennessee, but not Michigan, and Bush is able to hold South Carolina and take either Vermont, Kentucky, or Washington, but not Pennsylvania or West Virginia, away from Gore, then this thing is still up in the air. On the other hand, if Gore gets Vermont but not Tennessee, while at the same time Bush gets either North Carolina or Utah, and Maine defects to Canada, and—

REMOTE CONTROL: *CLICK*

DAN RATHER: It's butt-sniffin' time in the dog kennel folks, because this race is hotter than a weenie roast in a fireworks factory. This thing is tighter than a tadpole in a punch bowl. Calling this race is like baling hay in a snowstorm with a left-handed teaspoon. I feel like a man trying to give a frog a haircut with a harmonica. I feel like an alligator trying to put on a pair of sunglasses in a peanut factory. I feel like a pig trying to read a wristwatch in a barrel full of fried—

REMOTE CONTROL: *CLICK*

PETER JENNINGS: ABC News is now formally declaring that Al Gore has won Florida. ABC News knows this for a *fact*. You can trust us, because we're using a lot of high-tech computer graphics. When you see graphics of this magnitude, you *know* you're getting accurate information. Also, take a look at this suit I'm wearing. *Two grand,* this baby cost. So there can be no *question* that when I tell you Al Gore has won Florida, then—

REMOTE CONTROL: *CLICK*

TOM BROKAW: Tim Russert, I have just received word from my earpiece, which is connected directly to

Peter Jennings, that Al Gore has definitely won Florida. What does this mean?

TIM RUSSERT: Tom, it depends. If Gore can also pick up Oregon, Missouri, and any two states containing the letter "L," then he looks to be in very good shape. But if Bush is able to hold on in Georgia, Arkansas, and either Kansas or the British Virgin Islands, and then move his men northward to Gettysburg before Grant can position his troops, then—

REMOTE CONTROL: CLICK

DAN RATHER: CBS News is now saying that Gore won Florida, and when CBS News tells you something, you can take it to the bank. You can wrap it in pretty paper and tie it with a bow and give it to your momma. You can seal it in an envelope, put a stamp on it, and send it to the Internal Revenue Service certified mail return-receipt requested. You can put it in the oven and bake it at 375 degrees for 45 minutes or until a toothpick inserted in the center—

REMOTE CONTROL: CLICK

PETER JENNINGS: We here at ABC News have a minor correction to make. When we stated earlier that Al Gore won Florida, what we meant to say was, Al Gore did *not* win Florida. Is everybody clear on that? Also, I did not pay full price for this suit. But other than that we here at ABC News stand 100 percent behind every single word we—

REMOTE CONTROL: CLICK

TIM RUSSERT: Tom, now that we have taken Florida *away* from Gore, that changes the whole picture, because now if New York, Vermont, and Lake Erie go for Gore, but Indiana picks Bush and a candidate to be named later, and then Missouri decides to go to its nickel defensive package and blitz on third down, then quite honestly this thing could be too close to—

REMOTE CONTROL: CLICK

DAN RATHER: Folks, we are redder than a baboon's behind. We're working like a hamster on a Thighmaster to figure out how the heck we got this Florida thing wrong. All we know is, the margin in this race is smaller than a speck on a tick's whisker. This race is like a turkey wearing a woodpecker's necktie with a squirrel in each pocket. Calling this thing is like a blind snake trying to catch a three-legged monkey with a five iron. I feel like a raccoon with mittens on trying to play hopscotch with a—

REMOTE CONTROL: CLICK

PETER JENNINGS: At this time ABC News is formally declaring that the state of Florida, which earlier this evening was definitely won by Al Gore, has now been definitely won by George W. Bush. We're really, really certain this time. There is *absolutely no reason* to question this call, because we have made totally 100 percent sure that—

REMOTE CONTROL: CLICK

TIM RUSSERT: Tom, with Bush winning Florida, the whole picture changes completely, because now if Gore is unable to hold on to Oregon, and this cold front over the Great Plains moves toward this low-pressure system over the Atlantic, and California and Arizona join together to form a new state called "Calizona," and Switzerland remains neutral, then this thing could be too close to call. But on the other hand, if Connecticut finds out that Iowa has been having an affair with Alaska while carrying the illegitimate child of North—

REMOTE CONTROL: CLICK

DAN RATHER: Folks, it's time to slop the hogs and put some kibble where the slow dogs can get it, because CBS News is now saying that George W. Bush has won Florida. And when CBS News tells you something, you can put the family jewels in it and bury it in the backyard. You can put steel-belted radial tires on it and drive it down Broadway. You can land it on Baltic Avenue and build three hotels. You can climb every mountain, ford every stream, follow every—

REMOTE CONTROL: CLICK

PETER JENNINGS: We here at ABC News have another, um, OK, we're not calling it a *correction*; it's more of a *modification*, to our earlier refinement of our earlier clarification regarding the situation in Florida. Our current position, here at ABC News, is that George W. Bush, who was previously declared the winner in Florida, which was previously won by Al Gore, is—and here I am referring to George W. Bush—no longer the winner in Florida, at least for now. We here at ABC News are absolutely certain of this, as far as we—

REMOTE CONTROL: CLICK

TIM RUSSERT: . . . so if we take Florida *away* from Bush, and if Virginia goes for both Gore and Bush, and this little piggy goes to market, but this little piggy stays home, then—

REMOTE CONTROL: CLICK

DAN RATHER: This thing is jumping like a ballerina
playing poker with her tutu on fire. This thing is
crazier than a briefcase full of wolverines. I feel
like a walrus trying on a girdle in a tub of Cheez
Whiz. I feel like a two-headed chicken trying to
ride a unicycle through a car wash with—
BRICK PASSING THROUGH TV SCREEN: CRASH

In summary, the TV news people totally screwed up.
I'm not saying that we in the newspaper business did
any better. Oh, we tried to get the story right: We were
in constant contact with our sources all night. The
problem is that our sources were (don't tell anybody!)
the TV news people. And it turned out that they were
all getting their news from the same source, which
apparently was the Psychic Friends Network.

So the bottom line was that, on the morning after
Election Night 2000, the American public was totally
confused. Nobody knew who the next president
would be, because nobody knew who had won the
state of (cue weird X-Files music) Florida.

A lot of people were very upset, especially people
in Palm Beach County, who were saying that they
had accidentally voted for Pat Buchanan, which was
clearly a mistake. Even Pat Buchanan admitted this.

"You'd have to be nuts to vote for me!" he declared. "Hell, I didn't even vote for me!"

The problem was the design of the Palm Beach
County ballot. It was a "butterfly" ballot, which gets
its name from the fact that it is confusing to anybody
who has a tiny, primitive, insect brain.

No, seriously, it was very confusing, as we see by
the following photographic reproduction:

THE PALM BEACH BALLOT

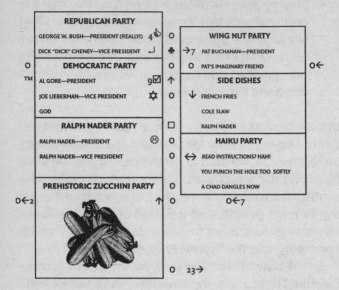

A lot of voters claimed they were confused by this ballot. Some voted for the wrong person; some voted for nobody[2]; quite a few voted for (why not?) *two* presidents.

Here's my theory about why the Palm Beach County ballot caused so much confusion: To use it correctly, *you had to be able to understand what arrows mean.* Unfortunately, a lot of Floridians, especially senior Floridians, have a *big* problem grasping the concept of arrows. Anybody who drives down here can confirm this. You'll be at an intersection, waiting in the left-turn lane, with a big painted arrow on the

---

[2]Actually, this was a pretty good choice.

street, pointing left; and a sign overhead saying LEFT TURN ONLY with an arrow pointing left; and then the light will change, and there will be a green arrow, pointing left, and 50 percent of the time the driver in front of you will do ... *nothing*. The driver has *no idea* what all these arrows mean. Sometimes the driver will attempt to turn *right*.

So I think the arrows were a big mistake. For the next presidential election, we should use a system that's less confusing, such as putting actual photographs of the candidates on the ballot. Voters could indicate their preference by using their hole-punchers to poke the candidate of their choice in the eyeball. Even then, we'd probably have problems. Some voters would become confused and poke out their *own* eyeball. And then they'd complain that they poked out the *wrong* eyeball.

But getting back to the 2000 presidential election: On the morning after, we still didn't know how Florida had voted, which meant we didn't know who would be our next president. It was a very unsettling time for the nation. The election had raised troubling questions—questions that threatened to undermine the public's faith in democracy. The only way to clear up these questions was for the two opposing sides to resolve their dispute by a process that was understandable, honorable, open, and fair. It took a *lot* of lawyers to keep that from happening.

Within hours after the first chad was dimpled, squadrons of lawyers for both sides had arrived in Florida. You couldn't throw a rock without hitting one (that was the only good thing about it). They were everywhere, filing lawsuits, making motions, objecting, stipulating, talking in Latin, and doing all the other busy-beaver legal things that lawyers do to prevent normal humans from having any clue what is going on.

They learn this in law school. I myself have never been to law school, but I think I know what goes on there: The students are attached to electrodes, then examined by their professors in a process something like this:

LAW PROFESSOR *(holding up a spoon)*: What am I holding in my hand?

STUDENT: A spoon.

LAW PROFESSOR: *(Presses a button.)*

STUDENT: AIEEEEEEEEEEE!

LAW PROFESSOR *(holding up the spoon)*: Again, what am I holding in my hand?

STUDENT: It . . . It *looks* like a spoon . . . NO PLEASE DON'T—

LAW PROFESSOR: *(Presses button.)*

STUDENT: AIEEEEEEEEEEEEEEEEEE!

LAW PROFESSOR *(holding up the spoon)*: Again, what am I holding in my hand?

STUDENT: In certain purely superficial respects, it may *resemble* what is sometimes called a spoon, depending of course on the definition of "spoon"; however, we intend to present expert testimony showing that there are a number of other plausible explanations, such that it cannot be determined beyond a reasonable doubt that this is a spoon, or, for that matter, *not* a spoon, per se, depending on who is paying us three hun-

dred dollars an hour plus expenses. Nor have we
established that, legally, that is *your* hand.

LAW PROFESSOR: Correct. *(He presses the button again
anyway.)*

Something like this *must* go on in law school, because of the way it changes normal people into people who refuse to make a simple, understandable
statement about *anything*. Before people go to law
school, if you say to them, "Nice day," they answer:
"It sure is!" After law school, they answer: "On what
basis?"

So when the lawyers got hold of the 2000 presidential election, it immediately stopped being
something that normal humans could understand,
and mutated into a complex intertwined mass of
incomprehensible court proceedings. These were
broadcast live on TV, with expert analysis provided by
lawyers who apparently just sit around in TV studios
with their makeup on, waiting for historic trials to
analyze. It was a confusing time, for layperson TV
viewers:

ANCHOR PERSON: In a moment we will be going live
to the courtroom of Judge A. Earl Frinkington,
Jr., who is hearing the appeal of the reversal of
the overturning of the denial of the injunction
against Judge Frinkington's previous ruling regarding the decision of election officials in
Caramba County to count ballots marked only
by specks of drool. As you can tell by the hushed
tone I am using, this is a very historic case that
could very well affect the direction of our live

coverage for the rest of the afternoon. We turn now to our expert legal analyst, Norman Twinkleboner. Norm, legally, what is about to transpire here?

EXPERT LEGAL ANALYST: Bob, in this hearing, the Gore attorneys must convince Judge Frinkington that they have established a case of *mandamus certiorari* with respect to the writ of *res ipso facto non compost mentis*.

ANCHOR PERSON: Can you put that in layperson's terms for our viewers?

EXPERT LEGAL ANALYST: No.

ANCHOR PERSON: OK, the judge is entering the courtroom. Let's listen in . . .

BAILIFF: Hear ye! Hear ye! Everybody listen up! The Honorable Judge Frinkington is on the scene! No chewing of gum!

JUDGE: Are the competing lawyers on hand?

LAWYER: Your honor, I am F. Pierpont Granule, for the defendant.

LAWYER: Your honor, I am Nedley M. Peesnicket, Jr., for the plaintiff.

LAWYER: Your honor, I am Walter Norkle for the decedent, hereinafter referred to as the mortgagee.

JUDGE: And you are all wearing wing tips?

LAWYERS: We are, your honor.

JUDGE: You may proceed with the argumentation.

LAWYER: Your honor, for our first witness, the plaintiffs would like to call Jennifer Lopez.

JUDGE: Really? Is she here?

LAWYER: No, your honor. But the plaintiffs sure would like to call her.

(*Laughter.*)

LAWYER: But seriously, your honor, we call as our first witness Mr. Walter Glompitt.

BAILIFF: Raise your right hand. Do you solemnly swear to tell the truth, the whole truth, a big old wad of truth, step on a crack and break your mother's back?

WITNESS: I do.

BAILIFF: You may kiss the bride.

LAWYER: Mr. Glompitt, can you state your name for the court?

WITNESS: Sure.

LAWYER: Objection, your honor! Hearsay!

LAWYER: How is that hearsay?

LAWYER: I heard him say it!

(*Laughter.*)

JUDGE: Sustained.

LAWYER: Now Mr. Glompitt, on or about the night of November 7, is it or is it not your understanding that, with respect to the matter at hand, and here I am referring to Exhibits 3986-A and 3986-B, to the best of your recollection, did you or did you not—

LAWYER: Objection!

JUDGE: On what grounds?

LAWYER: It sounded like he was about to complete a sentence.

JUDGE: The jury will disregard it.

BAILIFF: We don't have a jury.

JUDGE: Well get one, dammit!

LAWYER: Let me rephrase the question. Mr. Glompitt, can you tell the court whether, to the best of your recollection, on or about the night of November 7, with reference to Exhibits 3986-A and

3986-B, it would not be inaccurate to state that it is or is not your understanding that, insofar as the matter at hand is concerned, and taking into consideration the foregoing and, to the extent possible, the aftergoing, that it would not be an unfair mischaracterization to—

LAWYER: Objection, your honor! This is irrelevant!

JUDGE: Irrelevant to what?

LAWYER: I have no earthly idea.

JUDGE: Sustained.

LAWYER: Your honor, I don't see how I can represent the defendant when—

LAWYER: Objection! I'm representing the defendant!

LAWYER: Well then who am I representing?

JUDGE (examining some papers): You're representing the plaintiff.

LAWYER (smacking forehead): Shit!

(Laughter.)

JUDGE: The court will now take a brief recess so there can be expert legal analysis of these proceedings on TV.

ANCHOR PERSON (in hushed tones): We're watching live coverage of the historic proceedings in the courtroom of Judge A. Earl Frinkington, Jr. We turn now to our expert legal analyst, Norman Twinkleboner, for some expert legal analysis of what we've been seeing. Norm, what is your assessment thus far?

EXPERT LEGAL ANALYST: ZZZZZZZZZ

ANCHOR PERSON (louder): I said, Norman Twinkleboner, what is your expert analysis of this historic trial so far?

EXPERT LEGAL ANALYST (waking up): Bob, it's going to

boil down to whether the jury believes Johnnie Cochran's explanation of how O. J. Simpson's blood could have gotten on—

ANCHOR PERSON: Let's go back to the courtroom.

LAWYER: Now Mr. Glompitt, if I may resume the rephrasing of my question: With respect to Exhibits 3986-A and 3986-B, would it or would it not be incorrect to state, or, to put it another way, would it be correct not to not state, that on or about the night of November 7, is it your understanding—and when I say "your understanding," I mean it in the sense of "not your understanding"—that . . .

And so it went, hour after hour, day after day, week after week, an endless televised Attorney-a-Rama. By Thanksgiving, the American public had pretty much lost interest in the election and gone back to the mall. In the end, the Supreme Court could have declared that the forty-third president of the United States was Richard Simmons, and the overwhelming public reaction would have been: Thank God they finally picked *somebody*.

So to summarize: To avoid presidential-election messes like the one we had in 2000, we need to eliminate lawyers from the process, as well as television, stupid voters, and the state of Florida. I can't imagine anybody disagreeing with these simple, commonsense reforms. The only question is how we would go about implementing them.

I guess the first step would be to hire a lawyer.

Conclusion

IN THE INTRODUCTION TO THIS BOOK, I promised you that it would be inaccurate and poorly researched. I believe that I have more than lived up to that promise.

Still, there are some major issues that I didn't get to. For example: What should we do about Social Security? This is a big problem! A complicated problem! I had hoped to analyze it in great detail, with many statistics. But I'm out of room, so I'll try to summarize it with the following chart:

HOW SOCIAL SECURITY WORKS

YOUNG PEOPLE earn money, and send a hefty chunk of it to . . .	$→	the FEDERAL GOVERNMENT, which keeps a few hundred billion dollars for staff salaries, national defense, doughnuts, etc., and sends the rest along to . . .	$→	OLD PEOPLE, who use the money for living expenses, unless they already have plenty of money, in which case they spend it on . . .	$→ chew toys for their DOGS and CATS.

So basically, we're talking about a system whereby money is transferred from young people, via the federal government, to old people and their pets.

The problem is that the population is aging. Look at the cast of the TV show *Friends*. These people were young and charming once, but now that they're in their thirties, it frankly seems kind of pathetic and, yes, *weird* that all they ever do with their lives is wander in and out of one another's apartments.

Further televised evidence of the aging of the population can be found by watching the commercials during the evening news, which seem to feature nothing but products designed to enable old people to poop, keep their dentures on, or have sex. It's only a matter of time before somebody comes up with a product that does all three of these things simultaneously ("Try Polident-enhanced Ex-Lax, now with Viagra!").

Thus there are more and more old people in this country. The problem is, we're not generating enough young people to support them. Americans just don't have babies as often as they used to back in the old days, when the typical American woman churned out a baby every four or five months. Today, when a woman has a baby, she immediately enrolls it in a mother-baby play program, and a mother-baby music program, and a mother-baby aerobics program, and all these other mother-baby programs, so that, between schlepping her baby to all these programs *and* doing her job, she doesn't have time to have sex with her husband again until the baby goes to college.

So the bottom line is, we have too many old people in this country, and not enough young people, and the situation is getting worse. This means that the current Social Security system cannot keep working much longer. One solution to this problem would be for Congress to reform the system so that it makes economic sense. This is clearly the most logical solution, so we can safely assume that it will never happen. The current system is simply too popular with old people and their pets, who together form a large and powerful voting bloc.

As I see it, then, if we're going to solve the Social Security problem, we need to *increase the number of young people in this country*, while ideally at the same time we *decrease the number of old people*. How can we do this? I have come up with a practical, three-pronged Action Plan:

Prong One: We hire a band that makes hideously ugly music, such as Limp Bizkit, and we announce that this band will be holding a concert in, let's say, Nebraska, and that everybody in the entire world under the age of twenty-five can attend this concert for free.

Prong Two: On the day of this concert, we get every newspaper in the United States to print coupons that are good for one free entrée, on that day only, for any person over age sixty-five at any restaurant in Canada or Mexico.

What would happen, of course, is that millions of young foreigners would pour into the United States, while simultaneously a giant caravan of senior citizens driving 1987 Oldsmobiles would be leaving. We would wait for the exactly right moment, and then execute:

Prong Three: We permanently close the borders.

What do you think? It may not be a perfect plan, but I guarantee you it's better than anything Congress will come up with.

Another subject I had hoped to address in this book is U.S. foreign policy. I have some strong views on this subject, particularly concerning what we should do about "rogue nations," such as Iraq. I say it's time we stopped pussyfooting around. I say it's time we used the *ultimate weapon*. That's correct. As shocking as it may sound, I am proposing that if Iraq gives us any more trouble, we have an Air Force bomber fly directly over downtown Baghdad, open the bomb doors, and drop: Lawyers.

Think about it! Even a small number of American lawyers would probably paralyze a nation the size of Iraq within hours. And if the first attack wasn't enough, we could drop more lawyers. And if that wasn't enough, *we could put parachutes on the lawyers.* A cruel tactic, you say? Perhaps, but sometimes cruelty is called for.

Anyway, these are just a couple of the issues that I had hoped to analyze in this book, but, as I say, I am out of space. So in conclusion, let me just say: Thank you for reading this book, and if I said anything in here—anything at all—that offended you, I am truly, from the bottom of my heart, sorry.[1]

[1] Not really.

I also want to state that, despite the sometimes critical tone of this book, I really do think that the United States is a great country. And despite the good-natured "ribbing" I have given to the U.S. government, in reality I have nothing but the greatest respect for our federal workforce, especially the decent, hardworking, and—in my opinion—grossly underpaid employees of the audit division of the Internal Revenue Service. Thank you.

ABOUT THE AUTHOR

The New York Times has pronounced DAVE BARRY "the funniest man in America." But of course that could have been on a slow news day when there wasn't much else fit to print.

True, his bestselling collections of columns are legendary, but it is his wholly original books, like this one, that reveal him as an American icon. *Dave Barry Slept Here* was his version of American history. *Dave Barry Does Japan* was a contribution to international peace and understanding from which Japan has not yet fully recovered. *Dave Barry's Complete Guide to Guys* is among the best-read volumes in rehab centers and prisons. And now, with his take on American politics, and, especially, Washington, D.C., he takes his place with de Tocqueville and Larry King as a truly infamous explicator on and commentator of the process by which we find, fund, and . . . (fill in your own four-letter word here) our pols and public servants.

Raised in a suburb of New York, educated in a suburb of Philadelphia, he lives now in a suburb of Miami. (Won't they let him into the cities? Read him on, for example, Miami, which played such a pivotal role in the last presidential election, and you'll understand why.)

He is *not*, as he often puts it so poetically, making this up.